Emotions at School

T0418181

For more than a decade, there has been growing interest in the role of emotions in academic settings. Written by leading experts on learning and instruction, *Emotions at School* focuses on the connections between educational research and emotion science, bringing the subject to a wider audience. With chapters on how emotions develop and work, evidence-based recommendations about how to foster adaptive emotions, and clear explanations of key concepts and ideas, this concise volume is designed for any education course that includes emotions in the curriculum. It will be indispensable for student researchers and both pre- and in-service teachers alike.

Reinhard Pekrun is Professor and Research Chair for Personality and Educational Psychology at the University of Munich, Germany, and is Professorial Fellow at the Institute for Positive Psychology and Education at Australian Catholic University, Sydney, Australia.

Krista R. Muis is Associate Professor and Canada Research Chair in the Department of Educational and Counselling Psychology at McGill University, Canada.

Anne C. Frenzel is Professor of Educational Psychology and Academic Director of the M.Sc. Program Psychology: Learning Sciences at the University of Munich, Germany.

Thomas Goetz is Professor of Educational Sciences and Chair for Empirical Educational Research at the University of Konstanz, Germany, and is Professor at the Thurgau University of Teacher Education, Switzerland.

Ed Psych Insights

Series Editor: Patricia A. Alexander

REINHARD PEKRUN,
KRISTA R. MUIS,
ANNE C. FRENZEL,
AND THOMAS GOETZ

Emotions at School

Routledge
Taylor & Francis Group

NEW YORK AND LONDON

First published 2018
by Routledge
711 Third Avenue, New York, NY 10017

and by Routledge
2 Park Square, Milton Park, Abingdon, Oxon, OX14 4RN

Routledge is an imprint of the Taylor & Francis Group, an informa business

Library of Congress Cataloging-in-Publication Data
A catalog record for this book has been requested

ISBN: 978-1-138-73309-1 (hbk)
ISBN: 978-1-138-73310-7 (pbk)
ISBN: 978-1-315-18782-2 (ebk)

Typeset in Joanna MT
by Apex CoVantage, LLC

Contents

Introduction

Holding an educational degree has never been of more personal, social, or financial significance than it is today. The countless hours students spend studying, attending class, completing projects, taking exams, and building social relationships translate into progress toward crucial life goals—goals that are attained via individual and collective achievement in school and college settings. Given the subjective importance of these settings, it is no wonder that they abound with emotions. Remember the last time you took an important exam? You may have hoped for success, feared failure, or felt desperate because you were unprepared, but you likely did not feel indifferent about it. Similarly, think of the study projects you have been working on. Depending on the goals, tasks, and social interactions involved, you may have enjoyed working on them or felt bored; experienced a sense of flow or been frustrated about never-ending obstacles; felt proud of the outcome or ashamed of lack of accomplishment. As such, self-experience suggests that a wide variety of emotions can be experienced in academic settings, and empirical research confirms that emotions are frequent, manifold, and often intense in these settings.[1]

Emotions are both *experienced* in the school setting and *instrumental* for academic achievement and personal growth. For instance, experiencing enjoyment while working on a challenging project can help a student envision goals, promote creative and flexible problem solving, and support self-regulation. On the other hand, experiencing excessive anxiety about exams can impede students' academic performance, compel them to drop out of school, and negatively influence their psychological and physical health. The far-reaching consequences of emotional experiences are also likely reflected in the tragic numbers of attempted and committed suicides on school and college campuses each year.[2]

The importance of emotions in education equally extends to teachers and administrators. For example, teachers are responsible not only for imparting knowledge but also for inspiring passion for the discipline and excitement about learning. Of these outcomes, passion and excitement are the most elusive, because teachers often receive little training in the principles of affect and learning. This is even more so true for teachers and professors in higher education. If teachers succeed at inspiring excitement about the course content, the motivational benefits should extend far beyond the course itself. If they fail, however, the ensuing negative emotions, such as anxiety or anger, can quickly undermine motivation and the will to remain in the course or even in school.

Despite the clear relevance of emotions for education, emotions have traditionally been neglected by educational research—for a long time, educational research was almost exclusively focused on exploring students' cognitive learning and the cognitive outcomes of schooling. The only major exception is research on students' achievement-related anxiety, such as their test anxiety and mathematics anxiety, which started in the late 1930s and has flourished since the 1950s.[3,4] Whereas other disciplines—such as psychology, the neurosciences, economics, and many of the humanities, like history—experienced an affective turn since the 1970s, educational research continued to disregard emotions. Over the past 15 years, however, the number of studies focusing on students' and teachers' emotions has steadily increased and produced important initial findings.[5–9]

This book addresses the emotions experienced by students and teachers. The first chapter outlines conceptual issues, discusses the occurrence of emotions in academic settings, and depicts ways to assess them. In the second and third chapters, we discuss the impact of emotions on students' learning and achievement as well as their origins, regulation, and development across the K–12 and postsecondary years. The fourth chapter is devoted to teachers' emotions, and the final chapter outlines implications for educational practice.

REFERENCES

1   Pekrun, R., Goetz, T., Titz, W., & Perry, R. P. (2002). Academic emotions in students' self-regulated learning and achievement: A program of quantitative and qualitative research. *Educational Psychologist*, 37, 91–106.

2   Westefeld, J. S., Homaifar, B., Spotts, J., Furr, S., Range, L., & Werth, J. L. (2005). Perceptions concerning college student suicide: Data from four universities. *Suicide and Life Threatening Behavior*, 35, 640–645.

3   Chang, H., & Beilock, S. L. (2016). The math anxiety-math performance link and its relation to individual and environmental factors: A review of current behavioral and psychophysiological research. *Current Opinion in Behavioral Sciences*, 10, 33–38.

4   Zeidner, M. (1998). *Test anxiety: The state of the art*. New York: Plenum.

5   Efklides, A., & Volet, S. (Eds.). (2005). Feelings and emotions in the learning process [special issue]. *Learning and Instruction*, 15(5), 377–515.

6   Linnenbrink, E. A. (Ed.). (2006). Emotion research in education: Theoretical and methodological perspectives on the integration of affect, motivation, and cognition [Special issue]. *Educational Psychology Review*, 18(4), 307–405.

7   Pekrun, R., & Linnenbrink-Garcia, E. A. (Eds.). (2014). *International handbook of emotions in education*. New York: Taylor & Francis.

8   Schutz, P. A., & Lanehart, S. L. (Eds.). (2002). Emotions in education [Special issue]. *Educational Psychologist*, 37(2), 67–134.

9   Schutz, P. A., & Pekrun, R. (Eds.). (2007). *Emotion in education*. San Diego, CA: Academic Press.

One

Concepts and Measurement of Emotions

In this chapter, we explain how researchers understand the concept of emotion, and how emotions differ from terms such as "mood" and "affect." We also consider different types of emotions that are especially important in the academic context, such as achievement, epistemic, and social emotions. Subsequently, we address the occurrence of these emotions in academic settings and discuss how they differ between individuals and academic domains. Finally, we also describe methods used by researchers to measure these emotions. Throughout the chapter, the primary focus will be on students' emotions. The emotions experienced by teachers will be addressed in Chapter 4.

EMOTION, MOOD, AND AFFECT

It is generally accepted that **emotions** are multifaceted phenomena that involve several interrelated psychological processes. These processes include subjective feelings (affective component of emotion), cognitions (cognitive component), motivational tendencies (motivational component), physiological processes (physiological component), and expressive behavior (expressive component).[1,2] For instance, a student experiencing pre-exam anxiety may feel uneasy and nervous (affective), worry about possible failure (cognitive), want to flee the impending exam situation (motivational), have sweaty palms (physiological), and furrow her brow and pull her lips backward (expressive component).

The affective component is a necessary, core constituent of emotion. In contrast, other emotion components may or may not be present when an emotion is instigated. From a neuropsychological perspective, the affective component comprises an activation of subcortical brain structures (e.g., the amygdala) as well as feedback loops between subcortical and cortical structures that make it possible to experience an emotion as a subjective feeling state.[3] In comparison to emotions, **moods** are of lower intensity, have less-specific reference objects, and are typically of longer duration.[4] For example, if you enjoy the humor of a joke made by a friend, this would be considered as a momentary emotion, which can be quite intense but can be over after a few minutes. In contrast, if you are in a pleasant mood, this affective state need not be triggered by any specific event and need not be accompanied by any specific thoughts; rather, it can be in the background of your conscious attention and simply accompany you throughout your daily activities. Such a mood need not be intense, but hopefully it will last long.

Some authors define emotion and mood as categorically distinct phenomena—whenever you feel pleasant or unpleasant in terms of enjoyment, anger, or anxiety, this state falls into either the category of emotion or the category of mood.[5] Alternatively, since moods show similar qualitative differences as emotions (as in cheerful, angry, or anxious mood), they can also simply be regarded as low-intensity emotions.[6]

Different emotions and moods are often compiled in more general concepts of **affect**. Two variants of this term are used in the research literature. In the educational literature, affect is often employed to denote a broad variety of non-cognitive constructs including emotion, but also including self-concept, beliefs, motivation, etc.[7] In contrast, in emotion research, affect refers to emotions and moods more specifically. In this research, the term is often used to refer to more global variables of positive versus negative emotions or moods, with **positive affect** being compiled of various positive states (e.g., enjoyment, pride, satisfaction), and **negative affect** consisting of various negative states (e.g., anger, anxiety, frustration). For example, in experimental psychological research on mood, most studies have compared the effects of positive versus negative affect on psychological functioning, without further distinguishing between different emotions or moods.

Two important dimensions describing emotions, moods, and affect are **valence** and **activation**. Valence is defined by the degree of pleasantness, making it possible to distinguish positive (i.e., pleasant) states, such as enjoyment and happiness, from negative (i.e., unpleasant) states, such as anger, anxiety, or boredom. In terms of activation, physiologically activating states can be distinguished from deactivating states, such as activating excitement versus deactivating relaxation. Physiological activation involves symptoms like increased heart rate, increased respiration, sweating, speeding up of digestion processes, etc. Physiological activation serves to prepare the organism for quick reaction, as in flight when being anxious or as in attack when being angry. You can easily observe these symptoms in yourself when you are very excited, angry, or anxious. Deactivation, on the other hand, serves to put the organism at rest—sometimes to the extent that you fall asleep. The deactivation induced when you are bored by a task is a good example—when being bored, you start yawning, your body slackens, and your mind drifts away to the extent that you have difficulties staying awake.

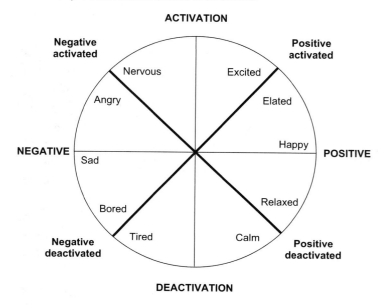

Figure 1.1 Affective circumplex

Model a dapted from Barrett and Russell[9]

Valence and activation are independent from each other: Different degrees of positive and negative valence can be combined with any level of activation, and vice versa. As such, affective states can be conceptually organized in a two-dimensional space. In **circumplex models** of affect, affective states are grouped in this way (see Figure 1.1).[8] By classifying affective states as positive or negative, and as activating or deactivating, the two dimensions can be used to distinguish four broad categories of emotions. The first group includes **positive activating emotions** such as **enjoyment**, excitement, **hope**, and **pride**. The second group includes **positive deactivating emotions** such **relief**, relaxation, and contentment.

The third group includes **negative activating emotions** like **anger**, **anxiety**, and **shame**, and the fourth group includes **negative deactivating emotions** like **boredom** and **hopelessness** (see Table 1.1).[6,9]

Valence and activation describe qualitatively different emotions. Another important distinction refers to the temporal generality of emotions: the distinction between **state emotions** and **trait emotions**.[1] State emotions are emotions that occur in a given moment, such as anxiety before an exam. In contrast, researchers use the term trait emotions to describe individual dispositions to repeatedly experience a specific state emotion, such as a student's dispositional tendency to often experience anxiety before exams. Along with other personality traits, trait emotions describe an individual's personality. For example, being a generally more relaxed or more anxious person is part of your overall personality. Trait emotions can be generalized across different contexts and settings, such as

Table 1.1 Three-Dimensional Taxonomy of Achievement Emotions

Object Focus	Positive[a]		Negative[b]	
	Activating	Deactivating	Activating	Deactivating
Activity	Enjoyment	Relaxation	Anger Frustration	Boredom
Outcome / prospective	Hope Joy[c]	Relief[c]	Anxiety	Hopelessness
Outcome / retrospective	Joy Pride Gratitude	Contentment Relief	Shame Anger	Sadness Disappointment

[a]Positive = pleasant emotion. [b]Negative = unpleasant emotion. [c]Anticipatory joy/relief.

general anxiousness related to various kinds of life situations. Alternatively, trait emotions can refer to specific settings, such as trait test anxiety, which is the disposition to experience anxiety specifically related to tests and exams.

ACADEMIC EMOTIONS

Emotions differ according to the events and objects that trigger them. Enjoyment is induced by positive events such as success on a difficult task, anger can be triggered by unfair behavior of a colleague, and anxiety can be caused by an impending exam. As such, emotions can be grouped not only according to valence and activation but also according to their **object focus**.[6] For explaining the psychological functions of emotions, this dimension is no less important than valence and activation. Specifically, regarding the influence of emotions on students' learning, object focus is critical because it determines if emotions pertain to the academic task at hand or not. In terms of object focus, the following broad groups of emotions and moods may be most important in the academic domain.

General and Specific Mood

Students and teachers may experience moods that lack a referent but that may nevertheless strongly influence their learning and teaching. Moods can be generalized, being experienced as just positive (pleasant) or negative (unpleasant), without clear differentiation of specific affective qualities. Alternatively, moods can be qualitatively distinct, as in joyful, angry, or fearful moods. While moods, by their very nature, may not be directly tied to a specific academic activity, they nonetheless have the potential to shape the way in which students engage in learning and teachers engage in teaching.

For example, when you are in a joyful mood, you may be better disposed to creatively solve a complex task than when you are in an anxious or angry mood. Similarly, a student in a good mood may be ready for attending to classroom instruction; a student in a negative mood may have difficulty focusing on the task at hand, thus limiting engagement.

Achievement Emotions

Achievement emotions are emotions that relate to achievement activities, such as studying and taking tests, and to the achievement outcomes of these activities—that is, success and failure (e.g., good versus poor grades). Accordingly, two groups of achievement emotions are **activity emotions**, such as enjoyment or boredom during learning, and **outcome emotions**, such as hope and pride (related to success) or anxiety, hopelessness, and shame (related to failure). Within the latter category, an important distinction is between prospective outcome emotions related to future success and failure, such as hope, anxiety, and hopelessness, and retrospective outcome emotions related to success and failure that have already occurred, such as pride, shame, relief, and disappointment. Many of the emotions experienced in academic settings can be classified as achievement emotions because they relate to activities and outcomes that are judged according to competence-based standards of quality.

In R. Pekrun's taxonomy of achievement emotions, these emotions are categorized along three dimensions: object focus, valence, and activation (Table 1.1).[6,7] The *object focus* of achievement emotions refers to the differentiation between activity and outcome emotions outlined above. In addition, as emotions more generally, achievement emotions can be grouped according to their valence and to the degree of activation implied (Table 1.1). In terms of *valence*, positive achievement emotions can be distinguished from negative achievement emotions, such as pleasant enjoyment of learning versus unpleasant fear or failure. For *activation*, physiologically activating achievement emotions can be distinguished from deactivating emotions, such as activating excitement about a novel task versus deactivating boredom during a monotonous lecture.

Past research on achievement emotions predominantly focused on outcome emotions. Two important traditions of research on outcome emotions are test anxiety studies and studies on the links between perceived causes of success and failure and subsequent emotions, such as pride and shame.[10,11] Though outcome emotions are of critical importance for achievement strivings, emotions directly pertaining to the activities performed in achievement settings (i.e., activity emotions) are also achievement emotions and are of equal relevance for achievement. The excitement arising from the commencement of a new project, boredom experienced when performing monotonous routine tasks, or anger felt when task demands seem unreasonable are examples of activity-related emotions. These emotions have traditionally been neglected.

Epistemic Emotions

The term "epistemic" is derived from ancient Greek. This term denotes thoughts and activities that aim to expand human knowledge, as exemplified by the pioneering thinking of the Greek philosophers. Thinking, however, is not just based on pure cognitive reasoning alone ("cold cognition"). Rather, it is closely tied to emotions such as surprise, curiosity, or **confusion**, which relate to the knowledge-generating qualities of cognitive tasks and drive the exploratory activities that are needed to expand knowledge.[12] For these emotions, knowledge and the generation of knowledge are the objects of emotions. This definition of **epistemic emotions** is equivalent to the definition of other types of epistemic variables that share the same object focus, such as epistemic cognition, epistemic metacognition, and **epistemic beliefs**. Epistemic emotions differ from these other epistemic variables by their affective nature.

Epistemic emotions represent a major category of human emotion serving evolutionary-based purposes of acquiring knowledge about the world and the self. A prototypical situation for the arousal of epistemic emotions is discrepant information and **cognitive incongruity**, which implies that different pieces of information are not compatible and do not fit together. A typical sequence of epistemic emotions induced by cognitive incongruity may involve (1) surprise; (2) curiosity and situational interest if the surprise is not dissolved; (3) anxiety in case of severe incongruity and information that deeply disturbs existing beliefs; (4) enjoyment and delight experienced when recombining information such that the problem gets solved; or (5) frustration when this seems impossible.[13] For example, a student who believes that climate change is due to natural causes but who is confronted with convincing information that a major part of climate change is human-made may be surprised and become curious about this information. Alternatively, the discrepancy between prior beliefs and current information may trigger confusion, and, if the incongruity continues, then this may be quite frustrating for the student. However, if the student is able to reconcile these different perspectives, she may be delighted by the solution she found.

Other terms for epistemic emotions are the concepts of cognitive emotions and knowledge emotions.[14,15] We prefer the term *epistemic emotions* because it is well established in epistemology and aligned with terms denoting other constructs related to epistemic processes, such as epistemic beliefs (i.e., beliefs about knowledge and knowing).[16] To conceptualize epistemic emotions, it is critical to attend to the defining features of emotion as outlined earlier. An affective state qualifies as an epistemic emotion if it comprises the affective, cognitive, physiological, motivational, and expressive components that define emotion. Accordingly, surprise, enjoyment, anxiety, frustration, and boredom related to knowledge and knowing can be considered epistemic emotions. This is also true for curiosity and confusion, which traditionally have not been classified as emotions but have been shown to involve affective feelings, physiological arousal, motivational impulses, as well as specific patterns of facial expression.[17,18]

Epistemic emotions differ from achievement emotions by their object focus. Knowledge and the generation of knowledge are the objects for epistemic emotions; in achievement emotions, success and failure are the objects. Some emotions are epistemic by nature, such as confusion, whereas others can belong to various categories of emotion, depending on the object focus of attention. Specifically, during cognitive activities, some emotions can be experienced as epistemic emotions or as achievement emotions. A student's frustration at not deriving a correct solution to a mathematics problem would be considered an epistemic emotion if the focus is on the cognitive incongruity resulting from the unsolved problem. However, if the focus is on personal failure and the inability to solve the problem, then the student's frustration would be considered an achievement emotion.

Topic Emotions

During studying or attending class, emotions can be triggered by the contents covered by learning material. Examples are the empathetic emotions pertaining to a protagonist's fate when reading a novel, the emotions triggered by political events dealt with in political lessons, or the emotions related to topics in science class, such as the frustration experienced by American children when they were informed by their teachers that Pluto was reclassified as a dwarf planet.[19]

In contrast to achievement and epistemic emotions, **topic emotions** do not directly pertain to learning and problem solving. However, they can strongly influence students' engagement by affecting their interest and motivation in an academic domain.[20] This is true not only for positive topic emotions but also for negative emotions—both pleasant and unpleasant experiences can catch students' attention and trigger interest. An example would be the disgust that children may experience at some kind of activities during science class, such as dissecting animals—an emotion that can stir students' curiosity despite its unpleasantness.

Social Emotions

Academic learning is situated in social contexts. Even when learning alone, students do not act in a social vacuum; rather, the goals, contents, and outcomes of learning are socially constructed. By implication, academic settings induce a multitude of **social emotions** related to other persons. These emotions include both social achievement emotions (such as admiration, envy, contempt, or empathy related to the success and failure of others) and non-achievement emotions (such as love or hate in the relationships with classmates and teachers). Social emotions can directly influence students' engagement with academic tasks, especially when learning is situated in teacher-student or student-student interactions. They can also indirectly influence learning by motivating students to engage or disengage in task-related interactions with teachers and classmates.

Similarly, teachers' professional activities are social in nature. Classroom teaching, interacting with colleagues, and giving advice to parents can elicit social emotions. Even if others are not physically present, such as during preparing lessons or marking exams at home, others are the targets of these activities. As such, teachers' emotions are inevitably social in nature as well. Examples are teachers' enjoyment of teaching students, their anger about students' lack of discipline, or their fear when being confronted with demanding tasks (see Chapter 4).

THE OCCURRENCE OF EMOTIONS IN ACADEMIC SETTINGS

Frequency of Different Emotions

What emotions do students experience at school, and how often do they experience these emotions? We have conducted a number of exploratory studies to analyze the diversity of emotions experienced by students. In these studies, we asked middle school, high school, and university students about their emotional experiences in three key academic contexts: studying, attending class, and taking tests and exams.[21] The studies used semi-structured interviews and questionnaires to explore students' emotions. In each of these interviews and questionnaires, students were asked a series of fixed questions and could give open-ended answers to provide qualitative narratives of emotional episodes. Video recordings of academic situations and psychophysiological analysis were also used in some of this research to facilitate and validate respondents' self-reports. In some of the studies, students were asked to recall typical academic episodes from their autobiographical memories and to report about the emotions experienced within these episodes. Other studies used a situated approach in which emotions were assessed immediately after specific academic situations. In both types of studies, we asked students the following simple question: "How did you feel in this situation; which emotions did you experience?" Students' answers were recorded, transcribed, and analyzed using both qualitative and quantitative methods.

As expected, the results showed that students experience a wide variety of emotions in academic settings. All major human emotions—save for disgust—were reported in students' narratives. Anxiety, in particular, was reported most often and constituted 15–27% of all emotional episodes across all three academic situations (i.e., studying, during class, during tests and exams). The pervasiveness of anxiety found in our research corroborates the importance of test anxiety research and underscores the high-stakes climate of school and college—factors that may pose serious threats to students' psychological health and well-being. At the same time, however, the findings suggest that the vast majority of emotions experienced in academic settings pertain to emotion categories other than anxiety. Overall, positive emotions (e.g., enjoyment, satisfaction, hope, pride, and relief) and negative emotions (e.g., anger, anxiety, shame, and boredom) were reported with equal frequency. Students also mentioned less frequently experienced emotions like hopelessness as well as social emotions like gratitude, admiration, contempt, and envy.

The relative frequencies of emotions differed across the three types of academic situations. During classroom instruction and studying, positive emotions accounted for slightly more than 50% of reported emotions, whereas during test taking, negative emotions outweighed positive emotions. Typically, attending class and studying involve less pressure for achievement and more autonomy for self-regulation than writing an exam, which may explain these differential frequencies. Table 1.2 provides some typical examples for students' answers related to emotions during exams. These examples are from a study in which we interviewed 54 student teachers who took their final university exams. We interviewed the students right after they had taken one of their oral exams, and we asked them how they had felt during the exam.[22]

The findings from our exploratory research thus confirm that the school and college experience is pervaded by a rich diversity of emotions (also see [2,23]). However, there may be

Table 1.2 Student Answers to the Question: "How Did You Feel During the Exam?"

Student Report	Coded Emotion
"When I was asked this exam question (. . .) I thought to myself, 'super, I know that (. . .),' and I was happy" (S 12)	Joy
"(. . .) this makes you feel enthusiastic (. . .) it's kind of a hidden joy (. . .) of course, you can't show it this way, they would think you're crazy" (S 8/6)	Joy
"And then my hope was he would continue asking questions on this subject, since this is material (. . .) I feel I know" (S 8/3)	Hope

Student Report	Coded Emotion
(At the beginning of the exam) "... I thought, that's a question I can answer, that's straightforward (...). And I was sure I could say something about it. This was kind of a relief (...)" (S 4/1)	Relief
"(...) I thought to myself, oh my god, again, one of the things you didn't prepare for, I didn't learn this stuff, and I got panicky (...)" (S 24/1)	Anxiety
"I am sitting there, getting anxious, thought to myself, 'I don't know that' (...) and, I don't know, blackout, probably (...). I was no longer concentrating. I couldn't listen any longer (...). I only kept thinking, 'Let's hope there'll be some questions I can answer'" (S 9/2)	Anxiety
"(...) he then kept asking questions on this material. I almost became desperate (...). I got a bit irritated then (...). Because I thought, why the hell is he asking for all these details, when I prepared for something else (...)" (S 9/3)	Anger (other-Directed)
"I was angry because I knew 'achievement' is a topic I know something about, but due to my disorientation, I won't be able to sell it the way I could" (S 26/1)	Anger (self-Directed)
"I don't like to let myself be embarrassed, but I really thought, if I don't manage to say anything about Piaget, nobody could help me any longer (...) I mean, this really is a bit embarrassing" (S 26/6)	Shame
"(...) this thought of resignation (...). I noticed, it doesn't go well, and then I even felt freed, because the expectations were gone" (S 15/4)	Resignation

limits to the generalizability of these findings. Emotions that are experienced less intensely may be underreported in any self-report assessment of emotions, since self-report relies on the availability of emotional episodes in situational or long-term memories. Also, culturally defined rules regarding reporting about emotions may play a role, perhaps implying that emotions like contempt or envy are experienced more frequently than acknowledged by participants in self-report studies. Furthermore, our studies used samples of German students; thus, these findings pertain to emotions experienced within German educational institutions. Education systems share many features across countries, but there also are differences that may limit the cross-cultural generalizability of the findings. More exploratory and base-rate research on the emotions experienced by students in different countries is clearly warranted.

Differences Between Individuals and Academic Domains

Emotions differ widely between individuals. This is also true for students' emotions in academic settings—different students can experience different emotions, even in the same situation. For example, one student may be excited when doing today's homework assignment in mathematics, whereas another student feels frustrated. These individual differences can relate to culture, ethnicity, gender, school membership, and class membership. For example, research has shown that average test anxiety is relatively high in students from some East Asian and Arab countries, as compared with students from Western countries.[10] It has also been shown that average test anxiety is higher in female than in male students (see Chapter 3 for an explanation of gender differences).

However, caution needs to be exerted in interpreting these findings. The differences in emotions experienced by different students within one culture are larger than the differences between cultures. Similarly, the differences among female students, and the differences among male students, are larger than the differences between the two genders. The same is true for ethnicity, school membership, and class membership. Most of the differences between students are due to the uniqueness of students' individual emotions and cannot be explained by group membership.

Students can also differ in how they react emotionally to different school subjects. For example, one student may enjoy mathematics but be bored by language instruction, whereas another student may be the opposite—bored by math but enjoy languages. The emotions experienced in similar subjects (such as mathematics and science) are often similar, but the emotions experienced in dissimilar subjects (such as mathematics versus languages) can be quite different. The differences between emotions in different school subjects become larger as students progress in education, and the differences are most evident in high-school students. In fact, in the senior high school years, correlations of emotions across school subjects tend to be zero, suggesting strong domain specificity of academic emotions.[24]

To explain, a correlation represents a statistical association between two variables. Zero correlations imply that all combinations of high and low levels of the two variables can occur: high/high, high/low, low/high, and low/low—such as high math enjoyment combined with high or low verbal enjoyment, as well as low math enjoyment combined with high or low verbal enjoyment. The reason for the differences of emotions across different subjects is that students' self-confidence and interests often vary across subjects. Therefore, emotions that are influenced by self-confidence and interest, such as enjoyment of learning or anxiety, can vary as well.

ASSESSMENT OF ACADEMIC EMOTIONS

Exploratory research using qualitative interviews with students and teachers is suited to investigate the occurrence and subjective phenomenology of emotions. However, more rigorous quantitative methodology is needed to gather more precise evidence on their functions, origins, and development. To begin such an endeavor, measurement instruments are needed. Given that emotions comprise multiple different components as outlined earlier, various methods that measure these components can be used to assess emotions. Examples are self-report questionnaires that assess the intensity and frequency of students' and teachers' emotions; measures of emotional physiological arousal as indicated by cardio-vascular parameters (e.g., heart rate), respiration rate, or the activity of sweat glands; neuro-imaging measuring the activation of brain systems recruited by emotions; and observation of emotional expression in terms of facial, gestural, and postural expression as well as prosodic (i.e., nonverbal) features of speech.

Among these methods, self-report instruments became the most popular. They are easy to administer and easy to understand. Furthermore, emotional feelings and thoughts are subjective phenomena by definition; as such, self-report is indispensable to assess these core components of emotions. Researchers have made continuous progress in the development of self-report measures of academic emotions. Today, many of the available instruments show excellent measurement properties.

Most of these instruments focus on measuring test anxiety. More recently, however, instruments for measuring academic emotions other than anxiety have also been made available. In the following sections, we first address self-report questionnaires of test anxiety. We then discuss two recently developed instruments that assess a broader diversity of achievement emotions (**Achievement Emotions Questionnaire** [AEQ]) and epistemic emotions (**Epistemic Emotion Scales** [EES]).

Test Anxiety Questionnaires

Due to anxiety's long-standing prominence among researchers in psychology and education, the development of instruments assessing this emotion has made significant progress since the 1950s.[10,25] Test anxiety measurement has been at the forefront of research on emotion assessment in personality psychology and education. Self-report questionnaires comprising multiple items to assess anxiety are the most frequently used method. These questionnaires are easy to administer, show good measurement qualities, and are temporally adaptable, making it possible to assess both habitual emotional reactions to exams (*trait* test anxiety) and momentary emotional reactions (*state* test anxiety). They comprise items assessing various anxiety-related emotional responses, and they ask students how frequently or intensely they experience these responses before or during tests and exams.

The first questionnaire to systematically assess students' test anxiety was developed by C. Brown at the University of Chicago in the 1930s.[26] Arguing that examinations had become increasingly important with the growth of universities, the change from small classes to large lectures, and the replacement of performance assessments based on classroom interaction by large-scale exams, Brown wanted to assess frequency and group differences in university students' exam-related anxiety. To this end, he constructed a questionnaire that comprised 70 items assessing affective, cognitive, physiological, and behavioral indicators of anxiety (e.g., "Are you nervous before an examination?"; "Do you worry about an examination the night before?"; "Are your hands wet and clumsy during an examination?"). Answers were provided on a five-point frequency scale (1 = *always* to 5 = *never*). Brown showed that this instrument was reliable (i.e., the amount of measurement error was small) and able to differentiate between groups of students.

Despite this success, Brown's questionnaire did not gain widespread acceptance. One possible reason is that research on self-experienced emotions did not fit the behaviorist Zeitgeist of the time, which favored objective measures and the investigation of observable behavior. This was different with G. Mandler and S. B. Sarason's **Test Anxiety Questionnaire** (TAQ).[27] Mandler and Sarason conceptualized test-related anxiety in terms of drives, and they posited that anxiety influences cognitive performance by triggering task-relevant and task-irrelevant behavioral responses. To test these propositions, they developed a scale with 37 items assessing affective, physiological, cognitive, and motivational components of test-related anxiety. The reliability of the scale proved to be good, and validity was shown by significant linkages between scale scores and intelligence test performance. Due to its theoretical underpinnings and measurement quality, this instrument became the progenitor of many of the questionnaires developed in the six decades that followed.

Similar to Brown's questionnaire, the TAQ comprised one single scale, thus assuming that test anxiety is a homogenous, one-dimensional phenomenon. Other scales that followed shared the assumption of unidimensionality. Progress was made when these scales were subjected to tests of dimensionality. The findings suggested that test anxiety indeed comprises more than one dimension. Based on these findings, R. Liebert and L. Morris proposed distinguishing between cognitive components of test anxiety, such as worry and lack of self-confidence (referred to as "**worry**"), on the one hand, and autonomic arousal (referred to as "**emotionality**"), on the other hand.[28] They used items from the TAQ to construct separate five-item scales for worry and emotionality, and they found that these scales showed different links to students' performance expectancies; worry related negatively to expectancy of success, whereas emotionality proved unrelated to expectancy.

Research has consistently confirmed that it is possible to distinguish between affective-physiological and cognitive components of test anxiety and that these components show different relations with performance-related variables, including students' academic achievement.[10,25] Typically, worries are more closely linked to performance because they relate to possible failure and its consequences. Emotionality, in terms of anxious physiological arousal, is less closely linked to students' performance. Consequently, researchers have developed two-dimensional instruments that use as their foundation the worry-emotionality distinction. Among these instruments, C. Spielberger's **Test Anxiety Inventory** (TAI) became the most popular.[29] The TAI was adapted for use in different languages, and for many years this instrument was employed in the vast majority of test anxiety studies.

However, subsequent studies have demonstrated that it is useful to further refine the worry-emotionality distinction—a shift that is in line with current multi-component definitions of emotion as outlined at the outset. An important advancement came with I. G. Sarason's **Reactions to Tests** (RTT) instrument that decomposed both the emotionality and the worry dimensions.[30] The RTT instrument contains 40 items organized in four scales measuring affective components ("Tension"), physiological components ("Bodily Reactions"), and cognitive components ("Worry", "Task-Irrelevant Thinking") of test anxiety. Each of the four scales contains ten items (e.g., "I feel distressed and uneasy before tests"; "Before taking a test, I worry about failure"; "During tests, I find myself thinking of things unrelated to the material being tested"). The scales showed good measurement properties.

Subsequently, a number of multi-dimensional test anxiety scales were developed that used Sarason's conception or a variant of it, such as the test anxiety scale from Pekrun et al.'s *Achievement Emotions Questionnaire* (AEQ), which will be discussed below. Today, researchers can choose between dozens of validated instruments assessing this particular emotion and its components. Furthermore, principles of constructing test anxiety measures have been used to create measures for other types of achievement anxiety as well, such as students' anxiety related to language classes (e.g., foreign language anxiety) or mathematics (math anxiety; e.g., *Mathematics Anxiety Rating Scale* [MARS]).[31] The sophistication achieved in anxiety measurement has enabled research on achievement-related anxiety to successfully analyze the effects and developmental trajectories of this emotion and to analyze the outcomes of treatments against its crippling effects.

Assessing Diverse Achievement Emotions: The Achievement Emotions Questionnaire (AEQ)

As outlined earlier, students experience a wide variety of emotions while engaging in key academic contexts (i.e., studying, attending class, taking tests and exams). However, measures of students' emotions other than test anxiety are still largely lacking. Attending to this deficit, we used the findings from our exploratory research mentioned earlier to construct a multi-dimensional instrument to measure a variety of major achievement emotions, including test anxiety as well as other achievement emotions (*Achievement Emotions Questionnaire* [AEQ]).[32]

In its original version, the AEQ is a self-report instrument that assesses college students' achievement emotions. The instrument measures a number of discrete emotions for each of the three main categories of academic situations: attending class, studying, and taking exams. Because these situations differ in terms of functions and social structures, the emotions pertaining to these situations can also differ. For example, enjoyment of classroom instruction should be differentiated from the enjoyment experienced during a challenging exam—some students may be excited when going to class; others when writing exams. Therefore, the AEQ provides separate scales for class-related, learning-related, and test-related emotions.

By varying the instructions accordingly, the AEQ is able to assess students' general emotional reactions in academic situations (*trait* achievement emotions), emotional reactions in a specific course or domain (*course/domain-specific* achievement emotions), or emotions at a specific time-point (*state* achievement emotions). In its current version, the AEQ can be used to assess eight different class-related emotions, eight learning-related emotions, and eight test emotions. Specific emotions were selected based upon reported frequency and theoretical relevance.

The class-related emotion scales include 80 items and instruct students to report how they feel before, during, or after class with regard to class-related enjoyment (e.g., "I enjoy being in class"), hope (e.g., "I am full of hope"), pride (e.g., "I am proud of myself"), anger (e.g., "I feel anger welling up in me"), anxiety (e.g., "I feel nervous in class"), shame (e.g., "I feel ashamed"), hopelessness (e.g., "I feel hopeless"), and boredom (e.g., "I get bored"). The learning-related emotion scales include 75 items and instruct students to report how they feel before, during, or after studying with regard to the same eight emotions as above. Finally, the test emotion scales include 77 items and instruct students to indicate how they feel before, during, or after taking tests and exams with regard to test-related enjoyment, hope, pride, relief, anger, anxiety, shame, and hopelessness. Within each section (class-related, learning-related, test-related), the items are ordered in three blocks assessing emotional experiences before, during, and after an encounter with the specified academic context. Sequencing items this way is intended to help respondents access their emotional memories.

The AEQ uses the same definition of "emotion" as cited earlier. As such, the items in each of the scales pertain to the affective, cognitive, physiological/expressive, and motivational components of each measured emotion. The scales of the AEQ are reliable and relate meaningfully to students' learning and performance. The AEQ predicts students' academic achievement, course enrollment, and dropout rates. Also, achievement emotions as assessed by the AEQ relate to components of students' learning processes such as study interest, achievement goals, motivation to learn, strategies of learning, investment of study effort, and the self-regulation of academic learning. Further, gender, social feedback, teachers' instructional behavior, and the composition and social climate of classrooms have also proven to be important correlates of the achievement emotions assessed by the AEQ.[32]

Epistemic Emotion Scales (EES)

Given the relevance of academic attainment for one's educational career and future employment, achievement emotions are critically important for students' academic agency. However, as outlined earlier, not all emotions occurring in academic settings are achievement emotions. Specifically, epistemic emotions that are instigated by the knowledge-generating quality of cognitive problems and mental activities are no less important for students' learning and performance. Surprise, curiosity, or confusion can profoundly influence students' interest and intrinsic motivation, persistence in investing cognitive effort, use of deep learning strategies, and ultimately their successful learning and long-term developmental trajectories. Initial empirical evidence supports the notion that epistemic emotions can facilitate knowledge acquisition.[33–36]

A self-report instrument that measures seven distinct emotions occurring during epistemic activities was developed by R. Pekrun, E. Vogl, K. Muis, and G. Sinatra (*Epistemic Emotion Scales* [EES]).[37] The EES contains 21 emotion adjectives that are organized in seven scales, including surprise ("surprised," "amazed," "astonished"), curiosity ("curious," "interested," "inquisitive"), enjoyment ("happy," "excited," "joyful"), confusion ("confused," "muddled," "puzzled"), anxiety ("anxious," "worried," "nervous"), frustration ("frustrated," "irritated," "dissatisfied"), and boredom ("bored," "dull," "monotonous"). Respondents are asked to rate how intensely they feel each emotion (1 = *not at all* to 5 = *very strong*). By varying the instructions, the scales can be used to assess either state epistemic emotions during single learning episodes or trait epistemic emotions occurring habitually during learning.

In a multi-national study on the role of epistemic beliefs and epistemic emotions for students' learning about complex and contradictory information related to issues of climate change (students from Canada, the United States, and Germany), the scales showed good measurement properties and predicted students' use of learning strategies and their learning outcomes.[37] The scales are available in the English and German languages.

CONCLUSIONS

Research has shown that students experience a broad diversity of emotions in academic settings, including both positive (pleasant) emotions (such as enjoyment, hope, pride, and curiosity) as well as negative (unpleasant) emotions (such as anger, frustration, anxiety, shame, confusion, hopelessness, or boredom)—there is next to no human emotion that could not occur at school. These emotions can relate to success and failure (achievement emotions), the topics of learning materials (topic emotions), the knowledge-generating qualities of cognitive activities (epistemic emotions), and teachers and classmates (social emotions). Alternatively, they can be brought into the classroom from events outside of school. Students differ widely in the emotions they experience, and their emotions can be domain specific by occurring in some subjects but not others (domain specificity of academic emotions). Various types of measures are available to assess these emotions, including self-report, behavioral observation, neuroimaging, and physiological analysis. Standardized self-report scales are the most widely used instruments to date and have proven reliable, valid, and cost-effective. Traditionally, these measures solely addressed students' test anxiety; however, instruments such as the Achievement Emotions Questionnaire have broadened this spectrum to include a variety of academic emotions.

REFERENCES

1   Shuman, V., & Scherer, K. R. (2014). Concepts and structures of emotions. In R. Pekrun & L. Linnenbrink-Garcia (Eds.), *International handbook of emotions in education* (pp. 13–35). New York: Taylor & Francis.

2   Quinlan, K. M. (Ed.). (2016). *How higher education feels: Poetry that illuminates the experiences of learning, teaching and transformation.* Boston: Sense Publishers.

3   Immordino-Yang, M. H. (2015). *Emotions, learning, and the brain.* New York: Norton.

4   Fridja, N. H. (1986). *The emotions.* London: Cambridge University Press.

5   Rosenberg, E. L. (1998). Levels of analysis and the organization of affect. *Review of General Psychology, 2,* 247–270.

6   Pekrun, R. (2006). The control-value theory of achievement emotions: Assumptions, corollaries, and implications for educational research and practice. *Educational Psychology Review, 18,* 315–341.

7   Pekrun, R. (2017). Achievement emotions. In A. J. Elliot, C. S. Dweck, & D. S. Yeager (Eds.), *Handbook of competence and motivation: Theory and application* (pp. 251–271). New York: Guilford Press.

8   McLeod, D. B., & Adams, V. M. (Eds.). (1989). *Affect and mathematical problem solving: A new perspective.* New York: Springer.

9   Barrett, L. F., & Russell, J. A. (1998). Independence and bipolarity in the structure of current affect. *Journal of Personality and Social Psychology, 74,* 967–984.

10   Zeidner, M. (1998). *Test anxiety: The state of the art.* New York: Plenum.

11   Weiner, B. (1985). An attributional theory of achievement motivation and emotion. *Psychological Review, 92,* 548–573.

12   Brun, G., Doğuoğlu, U., & Kuenzle, D. (Eds.). (2008). *Epistemology and emotions.* Aldershot, UK: Ashgate.

13   Craig, S. D., D'Mello, S. K., Witherspoon, A., & Graesser, A. C. (2008). Emote-aloud during learning with AutoTutor: Applying the Facial Action Coding System to cognitive-affective states during learning. *Cognition and Emotion, 22,* 777–788.

14   Scheffler, I. (Ed.). (1991). *In praise of the cognitive emotions and other essays in the philosophy of education.* New York: Routledge.

15   Silvia, P. J. (2010). Confusion and interest: The role of knowledge emotions in aesthetic experience. *Psychology of Aesthetics, Creativity, and the Arts, 4,* 75–80.

16   Hofer, B. K., & Pintrich, P. R. (1997). The development of epistemological theories: Beliefs about knowledge and knowing and their relation to learning. *Review of Educational Research, 67,* 88–140.

17 Reeve, J. (1993). The face of interest. *Motivation and Emotion, 17*, 353–375.

18 Rozin, P., & Cohen, A. B. (2003). High frequency of facial expressions corresponding to confusion, concentration, and worry in an analysis of naturally occurring facial expressions of Americans. *Emotion, 3*, 68–75.

19 Broughton, S. H., Sinatra, G. M., & Nussbaum, E. M. (2013). "Pluto has been a planet my whole life!" Emotions, attitudes, and conceptual change in elementary students learning about Pluto's reclassification. *Research in Science Education, 43*, 529–550.

20 Ainley, M. (2007). Being and feeling interested: Transient state, mood, and disposition. In P. A. Schutz & R. Pekrun (Eds.), *Emotion in education* (pp. 147–163). San Diego, CA: Academic Press.

21 Pekrun, R., Goetz, T., Titz, W., & Perry, R. P. (2002). Academic emotions in students' self-regulated learning and achievement: A program of quantitative and qualitative research. *Educational Psychologist, 37*, 91–106.

22 Spangler, G., Pekrun, R., Kramer, K., & Hofmann, H. (2002). Students' emotions, physiological reactions, and coping in academic exams. *Anxiety, Stress and Coping, 15*, 413–432.

23 Beard, C., Clegg, S., & Smith, K. (2007). Acknowledging the affective in higher education. *British Educational Research Journal, 33*, 235–252.

24 Goetz, T., Frenzel, A. C., Pekrun, R., Hall, N. C., & Lüdtke, O. (2007). Between- and within-domain relations of students' academic emotions. *Journal of Educational Psychology, 99*, 715–733.

25 Zeidner, M. (2014). Anxiety in education. In R. Pekrun & L. Linnenbrink-Garcia (Eds.), *International handbook of emotions in education* (pp. 265–288). New York: Taylor & Francis.

26 Brown, C. H. (1938). Emotional reactions before examinations: II. Results of a questionnaire. *Journal of Psychology, 5*, 11–26.

27 Mandler, G., & Sarason, S. B. (1952). A study of anxiety and learning. *Journal of Abnormal and Social Psychology, 47*, 166–173.

28 Liebert, R. M., & Morris, L. W. (1967). Cognitive and emotional components of test anxiety: A distinction and some initial data. *Psychological Reports, 20*, 975–978.

29 Spielberger, C. D. (1980). *Test anxiety inventory: Preliminary professional manual.* Palo Alto, CA: Consulting Psychologist Press.

30 Sarason, I. G. (1984). Stress, anxiety, and cognitive interference: Reactions to tests. *Journal of Personality and Social Psychology, 44*, 929–938.

31 Alexander, L., & Martray, C. (1989). The development of an abbreviated version of the Mathematics Anxiety Rating Scale. *Measurement and Evaluation in Counseling and Development, 22*, 143–150.

32 Pekrun, R., Goetz, T., Frenzel, A. C., Barchfeld, P., & Perry, R. P. (2011). Measuring emotions in students' learning and performance: The Achievement Emotions Questionnaire (AEQ). *Contemporary Educational Psychology, 36*, 36–48.

33 D'Mello, S. K., & Graesser, A. C. (2012). Dynamics of affective states during complex learning. *Learning and Instruction, 22*, 145–157.

34 D'Mello, S. K., Lehman, B., Pekrun, R., & Graesser, A. C. (2014). Confusion can be beneficial for learning. *Learning and Instruction, 29*, 153–170.

35 Muis, K. R., Pekrun, R., Sinatra, G. M., Azevedo, R., Trevors, G., Meier, E., & Heddy, B. (2015). The curious case of climate change: Testing a theoretical model of epistemic beliefs, epistemic emotions, and complex learning. *Learning and Instruction, 39*, 168–183.

36 Muis, K. R., Psaradellis, C., Lajoie, S. P., Di Leo, I., & Chevrier, M. (2015). The role of epistemic emotions in mathematics problem solving. *Contemporary Educational Psychology, 42*, 172–185.

37 Pekrun, R., Vogl, E., Muis, K. R., & Sinatra, G. M. (2016). Measuring emotions during epistemic activities: The Epistemically-Related Emotion Scales. *Cognition and Emotion, 31*, 1268–1276.

Two

Functions for Learning and Achievement

In psychological research, considerable attention has been given to the importance of emotions for human thought and action. In experimental studies, emotions and moods have been found to influence a range of cognitive processes that are relevant to academic learning, such as attention, memory storage and retrieval, and problem solving.[1–3] Much of this research, however, has focused on the effects of positive versus negative affect without drawing distinctions between specific, discrete emotions and mood states. This implies that it may be difficult and potentially misleading to use the findings for explaining students' emotions and learning in real-world academic contexts. Specifically, as argued in R. Pekrun's cognitive/motivational model of emotion effects, it is not sufficient to differentiate positive from negative affective states; it is imperative to also attend to the degree of activation implied.[4]

As such, it is important to distinguish between the four broad groups of emotions discussed in Chapter 1: *positive activating* emotions, such as enjoyment of learning, curiosity, hope, and pride about success; *positive deactivating* emotions, such as relief, relaxation, and contentment; *negative activating* emotions, such as anger, anxiety, shame, and confusion; and *negative deactivating* emotions, such as boredom and hopelessness (see Table 1.1). For example, both anxiety and hopelessness are negative emotions; however, anxiety is activating, whereas hopelessness is deactivating, implying that their effects on students' engagement can differ dramatically. Anxiety can motivate a student to invest effort to avoid failure, whereas hopelessness likely undermines any kind of engagement.

In the following sections, we first summarize research on the relation of emotions with different cognitive and motivational processes that are relevant to learning. We then outline how different emotions affect students' academic achievement.

THE INFLUENCE OF EMOTIONS ON LEARNING

Attention and Flow

Emotions focus your attention on the object of emotion. When you are enjoying music, your attention is focused on the music; when you are angry at a friend, you think about what your friend did to you; when you are anxious before an exam, you worry about possible failure and its consequences. Research has confirmed that both positive and negative emotional states use attentional resources by focusing attention on the object of emotion. However, attention is a limited resource—you cannot possibly fully attend to several different tasks at the same time, especially if these tasks are difficult or complex, which implies that each task requires full concentration. As such, consumption of attentional resources indicates that fewer resources are available for task completion, which can negatively impact performance.[5] To take anxiety again as an example: If students worry about possible failure while preparing for an exam, their attention is distracted away from the task, which will negatively impact their preparation.

Do emotions always disrupt task attention? Fortunately, this is not the case. The resource consumption effect is bound to emotions that have task-extraneous objects and produce task-irrelevant thinking, thus focusing attention away from the task. In contrast, in positive task-related emotions such as curiosity and enjoyment of learning, the task itself is the object of emotion. In these emotions, attention is focused on the task, and the attentional resources can be used for task completion. As such, these emotions promote total immersion in the task—a state that Cszikszentmihalyi calls **flow**.[6] When you forget about time, lose yourself in the activity, and nothing else matters, you are in a state of flow. Since attention is fully focused on the task in such a state, flow can boost your performance at learning.

Empirical studies with K–12 and university students have confirmed that negative emotions such as anger, anxiety, shame, boredom, or hopelessness during learning are associated with task-irrelevant thinking and reduced flow. In contrast, enjoyment of learning relates negatively to irrelevant thinking and positively to flow.[7,8] These findings suggest that students' emotions have profound effects on their attentional engagement with academic tasks. As a general rule, negative emotions distract attention away from learning, whereas positive emotions related to learning promote attention. However, the beneficial effects of positive emotions on attention do not generalize to any kind of positive emotion—if a positive emotion relates to other objects, it will distract attention away from studying, similar to negative emotions. As such, it is enjoyment of learning specifically that should be fostered. Inducing positive mood and a joyful atmosphere in the classroom per se is not sufficient to promote learning; rather, students' attention is sustained if learning itself is enjoyable.

Motivation to Learn

Emotions prepare us to do something. For example, negative emotions such as fear are warning signals that arise in response to events that can have negative consequences. Each of the major negative emotions is thought to be associated with distinct action impulses and serves to prepare the organism for action (or non-action), such as fight, flight, and behavioral passivity in anger, anxiety, and hopelessness, respectively. Anger prepares us for attack; anxiety motivates us to avoid the anxiety-provoking situation; hopelessness leads to resignation. For positive emotions, motivational consequences are less specific. However, an important function of positive emotions such as joy and curiosity is to motivate exploratory behavior, with the ultimate aim to enlarge one's action repertoire. Fredrickson called this the "broaden-and-build" function of positive emotions.[9] When in a good mood, we are ready for adventure and open to explore new horizons.

Due to their impact on motivation, emotions can profoundly influence students' engagement with learning. To better understand these effects, it is important to distinguish between two types of motivation. **Intrinsic motivation** is motivation to perform an action for its own sake—if you are motivated to study because you are interested in the learning material, you are intrinsically motivated. **Extrinsic motivation** is motivation to perform an action to attain outcomes. For example, if you are motivated to work hard to earn money, you are extrinsically motivated—it is the prospect of earning a salary that motivates you to work. Similarly, if a student works hard to attain a good grade and increase his chances for a successful career, the student is driven by extrinsic motivation.

Positive academic emotions—such as enjoyment of learning, hope for success, and pride of one's accomplishments—have been found to relate positively to students' interest and intrinsic motivation. Negative emotions such as anger, anxiety, shame, hopelessness, and boredom relate negatively to intrinsic motivation.[7,8] However, as detailed in Pekrun's cognitive/motivational theory of emotion effects, motivational effects may be different for different types of positive and negative emotions.[4] *Activating positive* emotions (such as enjoyment, hope, and pride) strengthen motivation, and *deactivating negative* emotions (such as hopelessness and boredom) undermine motivation to learn.[10] For hopelessness and boredom, these effects can be quite dramatic—these emotions can motivate students to drop out of school. In contrast, effects are more complex for *deactivating positive* emotions (such as relief, relaxation, and contentment) and for *activating negative* emotions (such as anger, anxiety, and confusion).

For example, relaxed contentment following success can reduce immediate motivation to reengage with learning contents but strengthens long-term motivation to do so. Regarding activating negative emotions, anger, anxiety, and shame have been found to reduce intrinsic motivation. However, these emotions can strengthen extrinsic motivation to invest effort to avoid failure, especially when expectations to prevent failure and attain success are favorable.[11] Similarly, confusion can be beneficial for learning, because it motivates resolution of the cognitive incongruity that produced the confusion. With confusion, motivating effects depend on the expectancy to ultimately solve the problem—if this seems impossible, resignation may follow. Due to these variable effects, the impact of each of these emotions on students' overall motivation to learn can be variable as well.

As with the effects of emotions on attention, this leads to the conclusion that it would be too simplistic to believe that positive emotion always fosters students' motivation to learn whereas negative emotions are generally detrimental. Rather, it is necessary to attend to the specific motivational functions of different emotions. However, with regard to positive effects, there is one emotion that generally supports students' motivation; this is students' enjoyment of learning.

Memory Processes

Emotions influence storage and retrieval of information. Two effects that are especially important for the academic context are mood-congruent memory recall and retrieval-induced forgetting and facilitation. **Mood-congruent recall** implies that mood facilitates the retrieval of like-valenced material. Positive mood and emotions facilitate the retrieval of positive self- and task-related information, and negative mood and emotions facilitate the retrieval of negative information. When you are in a joyful mood, you easily remember your strengths and successes. When you are in a depressed mood, you focus on all your weaknesses and failures. Accordingly, positive mood promotes positive expectations about the future; negative mood promotes negative expectations.

As such, mood-congruent recall can impact students' motivation. Positive mood can foster positive self-appraisals and thus benefit students' expectancies of success and resulting motivation to learn. In contrast, negative mood can promote negative self-appraisals, thus increasing expectancies of failure and hampering motivation.

Retrieval-induced forgetting implies that practicing some learning material impedes later retrieval of related material that was not practiced. This effect is likely due to inhibitory processes in memory networks. Such forgetting occurs with learning material consisting of disconnected elements. For example, after learning a list of foreign language words, practicing half of the list can impede students' memory for the other half. By contrast, **retrieval-induced facilitation** implies that practicing enhances memory for material that was not practiced.[12] Facilitation has been found to occur for connected materials consisting of elements that show strong interrelations. For example, after learning coherent text material, practicing half of the material leads to better memory for the non-practiced half as well.

Negative emotions can undo retrieval-induced forgetting. These emotions can inhibit spreading activation in memory networks which underlies such forgetting. Conversely, positive emotions can promote retrieval-induced facilitation. Positive emotions facilitate the generation and understanding of associations between different elements, thus promoting the relational processing of information underlying retrieval-induced facilitation.[13] This suggests that negative emotions can be helpful for learning lists of unrelated material, such as lists of foreign language vocabulary. In contrast, positive emotions should promote learning of coherent material, such as meaningful texts containing rich associations between different elements like objects in a science text or historical events in a history book.

Again, these effects suggest that one cannot assume that positive emotions are always beneficial and negative emotions always detrimental. Rather, the effects of different emotions are more complex—depending on the type of material, both positive and negative emotions can be beneficial or detrimental for memory storage and retrieval. However, if it is about learning material that is meaningful and coherent, enjoyment of learning is an emotion that should be generally beneficial.

Problem Solving, Learning Strategies, and Self-Regulation of Learning

Mood and emotions influence thinking and cognitive problem solving. Positive mood promotes flexible and creative ways of solving problems, and negative mood promotes more rigid, detail-oriented, and analytical ways of thinking.[14] For generating new ideas and hypotheses, being in a positive mood is most helpful. For judging the correctness of the generated ideas, being in a critical and less positive mood may be better. **Mood-as-information approaches** explain this finding by assuming that positive affective states signal that "all is well," implying safety and the discretion to engage in creative exploration, broaden one's cognitive horizon, and build new actions, as noted earlier.[9,14] In contrast, negative states are thought to indicate that something is going wrong, making it necessary to focus on problems in more cautious, analytical ways.

Accordingly, positive activating emotions such as curiosity and enjoyment of learning facilitate use of flexible, holistic **learning strategies**. Three typical examples of such strategies are **elaboration**, **organization**, and critical thinking. Elaboration of learning material involves relating the material to previously learned material in the same field or to material from other fields. For example, when learning about the civil war in the United States in the 1860s, students may relate the events to what they have learned about the preceding decades. Alternatively, they may reflect on how these events relate to principles of economy and how the economy of the states of the North and the South had contributed to the war. Organization of learning material involves structuring the material, for example by highlighting main ideas, reflecting upon connections between these ideas, and writing summaries.

Negative emotions, on the other hand, can sustain more rigid, detail-oriented learning, like simple **rehearsal** of learning material. When being in an anxious state of mind, focusing on just repeating vocabulary or historical facts may be easier than being creative and writing an open-ended essay. However, for deactivating positive and negative emotions, all of these effects may be less pronounced. Specifically, deactivating negative emotions, such as boredom and hopelessness, produce superficial information processing rather than any more intensive use of strategies.[10]

The effects of emotions on human thinking also have consequences for students' **self-regulation of learning.** In learning, self-regulation involves self-directed setting of goals for learning, selection of learning strategies, monitoring of the learning process, and judging the outcomes. Self-regulation of learning is a core twenty-first-century skill required to master the demands of lifelong learning and today's working world. Self-regulation requires cognitive flexibility—when deciding yourself what and how to learn, you need to be creative in setting goals and selecting actions. Because positive emotions promote flexible thinking, they also facilitate students' self-regulation of learning. In contrast, negative emotions, such as anxiety, have negative effects on self-regulated learning. These emotions promote external regulation by others, such as teachers or parents—when you are in an anxious state of mind, you may want to rely on external guidance.

EMOTIONS AND ACADEMIC ACHIEVEMENT

Since emotions influence students' attention, motivation, memory processes, and strategies during learning, they also affect resulting achievement. These links between emotions and achievement have been best researched for students' test anxiety. As outlined in Chapter 1, measures for test anxiety have been available since the 1930s. Researchers used these measures to assess students' anxiety, and they examined the relations between scores on these measures with students' school grades and performance on exams, intelligence tests, and academic achievement tests. Many of these studies assessed anxiety and achievement at the same time. This makes it difficult to determine their temporal ordering and the underlying cause-effect relationships—does anxiety affect achievement, are the links between the two variables due to effects of achievement (e.g., poor grades) on the development of students' anxiety, or are they explained by other variables (e.g., the influence of the parents)? However, researchers have also conducted experimental studies as well as longitudinal studies that assess anxiety and achievement multiple times in the same students. These studies are better suited to answer questions about temporal ordering and cause-effect relations. Furthermore, expanding on the existing anxiety studies, during the past 20 years researchers have also considered emotions other than anxiety, both positive and negative. In the following sections, we describe the findings of this research.

To organize these findings, we again use Pekrun's cognitive-motivational model of emotion effects (see Figure 2.1).[4] To reiterate, four groups of emotions are distinguished in this model: positive activating, positive deactivating, negative activating, and negative deactivating emotions. The model considers the effects of these emotions on students' attention, motivation, memory processes, and learning strategies discussed in the previous section. These components of learning processes contribute to determining if learning is successful or not, thus explaining the effects of emotions on students' academic achievement.

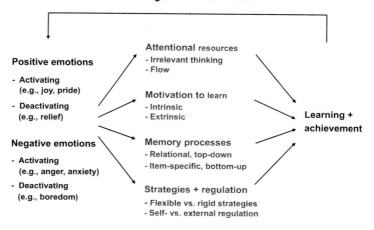

Figure 2.1 Effects of emotions on learning and achievement

Positive Emotions

In traditional accounts of positive emotions based on experimental laboratory research, positive emotions have often been considered maladaptive for performance. Positive emotions were thought to induce unrealistic optimism, foster superficial information processing, and reduce motivation to pursue challenging goals.[15] Some of the available experimental evidence seems to support such a view. For example, positive mood has been shown to (a) lead to illusionary probability estimates for favorable outcomes and an underestimation of the probability of failure; (b) induce relaxation and undermine effortful action by signalling that everything is going well; (c) induce motivation to maintain pleasant mood by avoiding negative thoughts and neglecting cautionary prevention of future adversities; and (d) reduce attention and cognitive resources needed for task purposes.

As aptly summarized by L. Aspinwall, traditional experimental approaches to positive emotions thus imply that "our primary goal is to feel good, and feeling good makes us lazy thinkers who are oblivious to potentially useful negative information and unresponsive to meaningful variations in information and situation" ([15], p. 7). However, as noted earlier, positive mood has typically been regarded as a unitary construct in experimental research. Such a view is inadequate because it fails to distinguish between activating versus deactivating moods and emotions. *Deactivating* positive emotions, like relaxation, can have the negative performance effects described for positive mood. As noted earlier, deactivating positive emotions can reduce task attention, can have variable motivational effects, and can lead to superficial information processing, thus making effects on overall achievement variable. For example, when you are in a relaxed mood, you may not perceive any need to exert effort to achieve, which implies that you will not perform at your best in such a mood. In contrast, *activating* positive emotions, such as enjoyment of learning, should have positive effects. Enjoyment focuses attention on the task, induces intrinsic motivation, promotes relational memory processing (i.e., activation of associations between contents in memory), and facilitates use of flexible learning strategies and self-regulation, thus exerting positive effects on students' learning and achievement. Activating positive emotions are especially helpful for students when tasks require flexible, creative thinking, such as elaborating learning materials, solving complex mathematical problems, and self-regulating learning.

The available research evidence supports the view that activating positive emotions enhances achievement. Specifically, enjoyment of learning has been found to relate positively to K–12 and college students' interest, effort invested in studying, elaboration of learning material, self-regulation of learning, and academic performance.[7] Furthermore, students' hope for success and pride about accomplishments also relate positively to these variables. Consistent with evidence on distinct emotions, general positive affect has also been found to correlate positively with students' cognitive engagement.[16] Despite these supporting findings, however, caution should be exercised in drawing conclusions for two reasons.

First, a few studies have found null relations between activating positive emotions (or affect) and achievement.[16,17] A likely explanation is problems with current self-report measurement of these emotions—using self-report questionnaires, it is difficult to clearly distinguish between activating enjoyment and deactivating, relaxed variants of this emotion. Second, most of the existing studies used cross-sectional study designs—that is, they assessed emotions and achievement at the same time. As noted earlier, the relations found in this type of research can be due to effects of emotion on achievement but can also be caused by effects of achievement on the emotion. For example, enjoyment can enhance learning and achievement, but achievement, such as success on exams and good grades, can enhance students' enjoyment of learning. When assessing enjoyment and learning multiple times in longitudinal studies, it has in fact been found that both causal directions play a role—students' enjoyment of learning and their achievement are linked by positive feedback loops, with each of the two being a cause as well as an effect of the other over time. Enjoyment and achievement are linked in a virtuous circle, each of the two promoting the other, thus contributing to a successful educational career and the motivation to engage in sustained learning across the school years.[18]

Negative Activating Emotions

Test Anxiety

The relationships of test anxiety with learning and performance have been analyzed in hundreds of studies.[19,20] Of these, four types of investigations are most prominent. In *group comparison* studies, the cognitive performance of low test-anxious students is compared with the performance of high test-anxious students. In experimental *test anxiety induction* studies, anxiety is induced by increasing the personal value (e.g., ego-threat) of an experimental task (e.g., by delivering failure feedback). In *cross-sectional* field studies, students' test anxiety is correlated with their academic achievement scores. Finally, in *longitudinal* field studies, the predictive relations between test anxiety and achievement are analyzed.

In *group comparison* and *anxiety induction* studies, test anxiety has been found to impair performance on complex or difficult tasks that demand attention and cognitive resources, such as difficult intelligence test items. Performance on easy, less complex, and repetitive tasks is either unaffected or even enhanced. Two arguments have been offered to explain this finding.[8] In *interference* and *attentional deficit* models of test anxiety, the effects of anxiety on cognitive performance are explained by the influence of anxiety on task-irrelevant thinking as described earlier—test anxiety involves worries about possible failure that reduce task-related attention and the efficiency of cognitive processing. An alternative hypothesis is proffered by *skills-deficit models*. These models suggest that test-anxious students suffer first and foremost from a lack of competence, which leads both to an increased likelihood of failure on complex tasks and to increased anxiety as a function of perceived personal deficits.

However, these two explanations are not mutually exclusive; rather, they complement each other. Both explanations are true: Test anxiety prompts task-irrelevant thinking, and the available evidence also shows that low-ability students are more prone to experience test-related anxiety. Furthermore, competence, anxiety, and performance are often linked by reciprocal effects over time: Lack of competence can induce anxiety of failure; anxiety can impair the quality of learning and performance; and low-quality learning leads to a lack of competence.

In line with experimental findings showing detrimental effects on cognitively demanding tasks, *cross-sectional field studies* have found that self-reported anxiety relates negatively to students' academic achievement. In comparison, the relationship between students' general anxiety and their achievement is weaker, since measures of general anxiety do not specifically pertain to the academic domain. However, for the anxiety-achievement link as well, caution should be exercised when interpreting cross-sectional relations in causal ways—it might be that relations between test anxiety and achievement are primarily caused by effects of academic success and failure on the development of students' anxiety, rather than by effects of anxiety on students' academic performance.

In fact, the evidence from *longitudinal studies* shows that test anxiety and students' academic achievement are linked by reciprocal effects across the school years. On the one hand, anxiety can impair students' learning and academic achievement; on the other hand, academic success and failure are prime drivers of the development of students' anxiety, with failure and poor grades exacerbating anxiety, and success and good grades alleviating anxiety.[18,21] As such, similar to the reciprocal links between students' enjoyment and their academic achievement discussed earlier, anxiety and achievement also are connected by feedback loops over time, with each of them influencing the other. In contrast to the virtuous cycles for enjoyment, the anxiety-achievement link involves vicious cycles, with negative effects in both directions that can aggravate anxiety and poor achievement over time.

A second reason for caution is that the relations of test anxiety with academic achievement have not been uniformly negative across studies. In some studies, anxiety and achievement were not linked, or even showed a positive relation. These findings point to the complexity of the anxiety-achievement relationship. In general, anxiety has deleterious effects in many students. However, as outlined earlier, it may induce motivation to study harder, and thus facilitate overall performance, in individuals who are more resilient to the devastating aspects of this emotion. For instance, *defensive pessimists* are found to experience anxiety when preparing for performance situations, and in response they set low expectations for their performance and extensively think through alternate plans and outcomes.[22] As a function of planning and envisioning possible outcomes, defensive pessimists appear to be able to manage and "harness" their anxiety, which is ultimately linked to better performance.

From an educator's perspective, however, any immediate benefits of anxiety are certainly outweighed by its overall negative effects on performance, interest, and intrinsic motivation in the vast majority of students. Despite differences in relative maturity and self-regulatory capacities, the available evidence suggests this should be equally true for K–12 and college students. Also, beyond effects on academic achievement, test anxiety can have severe consequences for students' long-term psychological well-being, social adaptation, and physical health, thus indicating an urgent need to ameliorate students' fear of failing in their academic careers.

Anger, Shame, and Confusion

While anxiety is the negative emotion that is most frequently reported by students, anger, shame, and confusion are three activating negative emotions that also occur frequently in academic settings. However, as yet these emotions have received less attention by educational researchers. *Anger* can be induced by many kinds of academic situations, particularly when students perceive barriers to goal attainment or well-being. Task demands that are perceived as being too high and grading practices that are perceived as unfair are frequent triggers of anger. Similar to anxiety, anger can involve task-irrelevant thinking and relates negatively to students' interest, intrinsic motivation to learn, and self-regulation of learning. As a consequence, it can also relate negatively to students' academic achievement.[7]

However, as with anxiety, the underlying pattern of functional mechanisms may be complex and imply more than just negative effects. For example, in a study with undergraduate students reported by A. Lane and colleagues,[23] depressed mood interacted with anger experienced before an academic exam such that anger was related to *improved* performance in students who did not feel depressed. Anger is detrimental for motivation and performance under many conditions, but it can translate into increased task motivation when expectancies for agency and success are favorable.

Shame is at the core of negative feelings of self-worth, often implying devastating, pervasive feelings of self-abasement. In traditional achievement motivation theories, shame was regarded as central to the fear-of-failure motive—anticipating shame was thought to motivate behavior aiming to avoid failure and perceptions of inability, such as selecting very easy tasks or very difficult tasks that most people cannot solve.[24] Similar to anxiety and anger, students' achievement-related shame is negatively associated with their achievement in most instances.[7] However, as with anxiety and anger, shame can exert variable motivational effects. For instance, J. Turner and D. Schallert showed that students who experienced shame following negative exam feedback increased their motivation when they continued to be committed to future academic goals and believed these goals were attainable.[11]

Finally, *confusion* is an epistemic emotion that occurs when cognitive incongruity cannot be easily resolved. Students experience confusion when they are unable to follow a lecture or to understand a cognitive problem. Confusion can also occur when students' epistemic beliefs (i.e., their beliefs about the nature of knowledge and knowing) conflict with the nature of a task. For example, believing that knowledge is certain and that scientists agree on important matters would conflict with information that scientists do not agree on a given matter (e.g., the causes for climate change).[25] The evolutionary purpose of confusion is to motivate individuals to solve the incongruity, which helps to better understand and manage the world. Accordingly, it has been shown that confusion about a problem can promote persistence in solving the problem and ultimately promote learning.[26] However, if the cognitive incongruity cannot be resolved, motivation can be replaced by frustration, boredom, and resignation, thus undermining progress at learning.

Deactivating Negative Emotions

In contrast to activating negative emotions, which can exert variable effects, boredom and hopelessness have been found to be generally detrimental to students' achievement.[27] These emotions promote task-irrelevant thinking, thus undermining attention and concentration. When bored, your mind starts wandering, and you may engage in daydreaming rather than focusing on the task at hand. Furthermore, boredom and hopelessness reduce both intrinsic and extrinsic motivation— being bored or hopeless, you are interested neither in the learning material nor in investing effort to attain success. Rather, you disengage from learning and task performance. Finally, these emotions also undermine any systematic use of learning strategies but promote superficial information processing. As a consequence, boredom and hopelessness prove detrimental for any kind of cognitive performance and derail students' academic achievement.[28, 29]

CONCLUSIONS

Emotions have been shown to profoundly influence human thought, motivation, and action. They direct attention, shape motivation, impact memory processes, and affect self-regulation. As a consequence, they also impact academic learning. Emotions focus students' attention on learning tasks or distract attention away, promote or undermine their motivation to learn, impact memory processes such as mood-congruent recall and retrieval-induced forgetting, facilitate different types of learning strategies, and help or hinder students' self-regulation of learning. Due to their effects on learning, emotions also impact students' academic achievement outcomes. Positive activating emotions, such as enjoyment of learning, typically exert positive effects on achievement, whereas negative deactivating emotions, such as boredom and hopelessness, have been found to undermine achievement. The effects of negative activating emotions (such as anger, anxiety, shame, or confusion) are more variable, due to their complex effects on different components of learning processes. However, in the average student, the impact of anger, anxiety, and shame on overall academic achievement is negative as well.

REFERENCES

1   Davidson, R. J., Scherer, K. R., & Goldsmith, H. H. (Eds.). (2003). *Handbook of affective sciences*. Oxford, UK: Oxford University Press.

2   Barrett, L. F., Lewis, M., & Haviland-Jones, J. M. (Eds.). (2016). *Handbook of emotions* (4th edition). New York: Guilford.

3   Pekrun, R., & Linnenbrink-Garcia, L. (Eds.). (2014). *International handbook of emotions in education*. New York: Taylor & Francis.

4   Pekrun, R. (2006). The control-value theory of achievement emotions: Assumptions, corollaries, and implications for educational research and practice. *Educational Psychology Review, 18*, 315–341.

5   Meinhardt, J., & Pekrun, R. (2003). Attentional resource allocation to emotional events: An ERP study. *Cognition and Emotion, 17*, 477–500.

6   Czikszentmihali, M. (1975). *Beyond boredom and anxiety*. San Francisco: Jossey-Bass.

7   Pekrun, R., Goetz, T., Titz, W., & Perry, R. P. (2002). Academic emotions in students' self-regulated learning and achievement: A program of quantitative and qualitative research. *Educational Psychologist, 37*, 91–106.

8   Zeidner, M. (1998). *Test anxiety: The state of the art*. New York: Plenum.

9   Fredrickson, B. L. (2001). The role of positive emotions in positive psychology: The broaden-and-build theory of positive emotions. *American Psychologist, 56*, 218–226.

10 Pekrun, R., Goetz, T., Daniels, L. M., Stupnisky, R. H., & Perry, R. P. (2010). Boredom in achievement settings: Control-value antecedents and performance outcomes of a neglected emotion. *Journal of Educational Psychology, 102*, 531–549.

11 Turner, J. E., & Schallert, D. L. (2001). Expectancy-value relationships of shame reactions and shame resiliency. *Journal of Educational Psychology*, 93, 320–329.

12 Chan, C. K., McDermott, K. B., & Roediger, H. L. (2006). Retrieval-induced facilitation: Initially nontested material can benefit from prior testing. *Journal of Experimental Psychology: General*, 135, 533–571.

13 Kuhbandner, C., & Pekrun, R. (2013). Affective state influences retrieval-induced forgetting for integrated knowledge. *PloS ONE*, 8(2), e56617.

14 Clore, G. L., & Huntsinger, J. R. (2009). How the object of affect guides its impact. *Emotion Review*, 1, 39–54.

15 Aspinwall, L. (1998). Rethinking the role of positive affect in self-regulation. *Motivation and Emotion*, 22, 1–32.

16 Linnenbrink, E. A. (2007). The role of affect in student learning: A multi-dimensional approach to considering the interaction of affect, motivation, and engagement. In P. A. Schutz & R. Pekrun (Eds.), *Emotion in education* (pp. 107–124). San Diego, CA: Academic Press.

17 Pekrun, R., Elliot, A. J., & Maier, M. A. (2009). Achievement goals and achievement emotions: Testing a model of their joint relations with academic performance. *Journal of Educational Psychology*, 101, 115–135.

18 Pekrun, R., Lichtenfeld, S., Marsh, H. W., Murayama, K., & Goetz, T. (2017). Achievement emotions and academic performance: Longitudinal models of reciprocal effects. *Child Development*. Advance online publication. doi: 10.1111/cdev12704

19 Hembree, R. (1988). Correlates, causes, effects, and treatment of test anxiety. *Review of Educational Research*, 58, 47–77.

20 Zeidner, M. (2014). Anxiety in education. In R. Pekrun & L. Linnenbrink-Garcia (Eds.), *International handbook of emotions in education* (pp. 265–288). New York: Taylor & Francis.

21 Meece, J. L., Wigfield, A., & Eccles, J. S. (1990). Predictors of math anxiety and its influence on young adolescents' course enrollment intentions and performance in mathematics. *Journal of Educational Psychology*, 82, 60–70.

22 Norem, J. K., & Cantor, N. (1986). Defensive pessimism: Harnessing anxiety as motivation. *Journal of Personality and Social Psychology*, 51, 1208–1217.

23   Lane, A. M., Terry, P. C., Beedle, C. J., Curry, D. A., & Clark, N. (2001). Mood and performance: Test of a conceptual model with a focus on depressed mood. *Psychology of Sport and Exercise*, 2, 157–172.

24   Heckhausen, H. (1991). *Motivation and action*. New York: Springer.

25   Muis, K. R., Pekrun, R., Sinatra, G. M., Azevedo, R., Trevors, G., Meier, E., & Heddy, B. (2015). The curious case of climate change: Testing a theoretical model of epistemic beliefs, epistemic emotions, and complex learning. *Learning and Instruction*, 39, 168–183.

26   D'Mello, S. K., Lehman, B., Pekrun, R., & Graesser, A. C. (2014). Confusion can be beneficial for learning. *Learning and Instruction*, 29, 153–170.

27   Goetz, T., & Hall, N. C. (2014). Academic boredom. In R. Pekrun & L. Linnenbrink-Garcia (Eds.), *International handbook of emotions in education* (pp. 311–330). New York: Taylor & Francis.

28   Pekrun, R., Hall, N. C., Goetz, T., & Perry, R. P. (2014). Boredom and academic achievement: Testing a model of reciprocal causation. *Journal of Educational Psychology*, 106, 696–710.

29   Tze, V. M. C., Daniels, L. M., & Klassen, R. M. (2016). Evaluating the relationship between boredom and academic outcomes: A meta-analysis. *Educational Psychology Review*, 28, 119–144.

Three

Origins, Regulation, and Development of Emotions

Given the relevance of emotions for students' learning and achievement, it is important to consider their origins, regulation, and development. Without such knowledge, it would not be possible for practitioners to address students' emotions in an evidence-based way, grounded in sound theory and empirical findings. Generally, emotions can be caused and regulated by many different factors. Variations in genetic dispositions explain some of the differences between students in terms of the emotions they experience, although not to the extent to which differences in cognitive abilities may depend on genes. For example, differences in levels of anxiety are influenced by genetic dispositions.[1] Situational perceptions give rise to emotions, such as the joy triggered by success and frustration induced by failure. Neurohormonal processes can influence the arousal of emotions, and use of substances, such as medical drugs or alcohol, can contribute to their effects. Sensory perceptions of one's expression of emotion in the face, gestures, and posture can feed back on the emotions that gave rise to the expression—showing an angry face can increase anger even if one does not look into the mirror. Emotion schemata stored in memory play a role; these schemata link specific stimuli to emotional arousal, such as perceptions of snakes causing fear due to the biologically prepared link between snakes representing threat and the evolutionarily adaptive reaction to avoid them.

For academic emotions, however, there is one group of factors that is likely more important than any other factor—individual appraisals of success, failure, one's competence, and the value of achievement activities and their outcomes. In contrast to emotions aroused in phylogenetically older and more constrained situations, such as enjoyment of physiological need fulfillment or interactions between caregiver and child, emotions in academic situations pertain to culturally defined demands in settings that are a recent product of civilization. In settings of this kind, the individual has to learn how to adapt to situational demands while preserving individual autonomy—a process inevitably guided by appraisals. In other words, in settings shaped by our cultural evolution, appraisals of the situation and oneself are necessary for adaptive thought, emotion, and action.

This becomes especially clear when considering transitions in students' educational careers, such as the transitions from kindergarten or preschool to elementary school, from there to middle school and further on to high school, or from high school to university. For example, the transition from high school to college often implies breaking habits developed during childhood and adolescence. Typically, this transition entails challenges to adapt to new academic demands; to leave one's home, move to a new city, and live on one's own; and to create new friendships and social networks. All of these changes make it necessary to appraise new situations and to re-appraise one's personal strengths and weaknesses, and these appraisals certainly play a major role in the emotions that students experience.

In line with such considerations, researchers agree that appraisals are primary antecedents of the emotions occurring in academic and achievement-related settings. Most theories and empirical studies on the determinants of students' emotions focus on the emotional relevance of self-related and task-related appraisals and on the importance of situational factors that shape students' emotions by influencing their appraisals. In this chapter, we first discuss theory and evidence on individual antecedents of academic emotions, including appraisals as well as more distal individual factors influencing appraisals and emotions, such as students' gender and their achievement goals. Subsequently, we discuss the role of **emotion regulation** and **emotional competencies** (called "emotional intelligence" by some authors) for students' emotions. We then describe the role of classroom instruction and social environments for these emotions, and finally we outline how they develop over the school years. Throughout the chapter, we will use R. Pekrun's **control-value theory** of achievement emotions as an organizing framework to explain researchers' hypotheses and the existing evidence.[2]

INDIVIDUAL ORIGINS OF EMOTIONS

Appraisals as Antecedents

Achievement Emotions

Much research on the individual determinants of students' emotions has focused on the origins of test anxiety. Test anxiety is a prospective emotion related to threat of failure on an upcoming or ongoing evaluation (i.e., test or exam). Therefore, many authors have regarded threat-related appraisals as the proximal determinants of test anxiety. For example, from the perspective of R. Lazarus's transactional stress model, test anxiety is based on two kinds of appraisals.[3] The *primary appraisal* pertains to the situational possibility and subjective importance of failure. In the *secondary appraisal*, possibilities to cope with the situation are explored cognitively. Depending on the combined result of the two appraisals, different emotions can be aroused. In the case of threat and insufficient perceived control over threatening failure, anxiety is assumed to be instigated. For example, when facing a difficult exam, you may first ask yourself if the exam is sufficiently important to care about. If the answer is yes, you may subsequently wonder if your abilities are sufficient and if you can prepare sufficiently well to succeed. If you deem the exam to be important and feel out of control because you feel you lack ability and are not prepared, you may feel fearful about the prospect of possibly failing the exam.

Lazarus's analysis suggests that test-related anxiety is aroused when two conditions are met. First, the upcoming test is deemed important. Second, the individual doubts whether her abilities and preparation are sufficient, thus letting her believe that she may fail the test. Research has confirmed that three related groups of appraisals are most important to predict if, and to what extent, a student is fearful before exams and in academic achievement situations more generally. The first is **perceived control** and the achievement expectations resulting from perceived control. Specifically, expectations of failure relate positively to anxiety—the more you expect failure, the more anxious you are. The second is **perceived competence**, such as students' self-concept of ability. By self-concept, researchers mean beliefs about one's abilities that are stored in memory. For example, your beliefs about your abilities in mathematics make up your math self-concept. Self-concepts of ability lay the foundations for expectancies of success and failure. As such, they relate negatively to anxiety—the higher your self-concept, the less you expect failure, and the less test anxious you are, all other things being equal. The third group of appraisals involves the **perceived value** of achievement, which relates positively to test anxiety—high importance of achievement exacerbates test anxiety.

Achievement expectations and self-concepts of ability define individuals' self-confidence to control their achievement. For some emotions, it is important to additionally consider another group of control-related appraisals: students' **causal attributions** of success and failure.[4] For example, whereas one student may explain failure by lack of ability, another student may realize that it was lack of effort rather than lack of ability that let him fail the exam. Students can attribute their successes and failures to internal factors, such as ability and effort (internal causal attribution); alternatively, they can believe that external factors are responsible, such as difficult task demands or luck (external causal attribution).

For appraisals related to self-confidence and perceived control, a broad range of different terms has been proposed. Examples include self-concept of ability, perceived competence, judgment of knowing, self-efficacy, outcome expectations, coping potential, power, agency, locus of control, etc.[5] Don't be confused by the Babylonian chaos of terms in this field—while all of these concepts show subtle distinctions that may sometimes be useful to consider, all of them broadly represent individuals' sense of self-confidence and control over achievement.

Together, these different appraisals explain the arousal of various achievement emotions, including both activity emotions and outcome emotions as described in Chapter 1 and addressed in R. Pekrun's control-value theory and related empirical research.[2,6] For *activity emotions* such as enjoyment of learning and boredom, perceived competence and value are most important. Enjoyment of learning is promoted when competence is sufficient to master the material and the student is interested in the material. In contrast, in cases of feelings of incompetence or disinterest, the activity is not enjoyable. Boredom occurs when the activity lacks value—when students perceive a lecture as monotonous or learning materials as disinteresting, thus not providing sufficient stimulation, they get bored. As for perceived competence and related perceptions of task demands, boredom can occur under either of two conditions. One is under-challenge defined by low perceived demands coupled with high perceived competence to master the task. This is typical for easy and monotonous routine tasks (such as assembly line work) and sometimes also is the case for gifted students in regular classroom instruction. The other is over-challenge defined by high perceived demands coupled with low perceived competence. The research evidence suggests that boredom promoted by over-challenge is more frequent in students than boredom due to under-challenge. Many students today are faced with task demands that are overly challenging or are given materials they do not understand, thus undermining their capability to make meaning and exacerbating their boredom.

Prospective outcome emotions that relate to future success and failure depend on achievement expectations, combined with perceptions of the value (i.e., importance) of success and failure. Hope is the primary emotion related to future success that is not certain—if you deem achievement to be critically important but are not fully confident that you will be able to attain success, you may be full of hope or at least feel a little sense of hope. The opposite negative emotion related to failure is anxiety. Achievement-related anxiety comprises fear of failure and is triggered by expectancies of possible failure, coupled with perceived importance of achievement, as outlined earlier.

Both hope and anxiety involve an element of uncertainty. As such, both can be triggered when either success or failure is the possible outcome of an achievement activity but one doesn't know exactly which one will occur. If the focus of attention is on possible success, hope is the emotion; if the focus is on possible failure, it is anxiety. Attentional focus can shift rapidly from one to the other, depending on situational triggers such as current progress in preparing for an exam. As such, students often experience an emotional roller coaster, with emotions oscillating back and forth between hope and anxiety.

However, if failure is subjectively certain and success not possible to attain, anxiety can be replaced by achievement-related hopelessness. As described in Chapter 2, hopelessness is a devastating emotion that can derail students' educational attainment and motivate them to drop out of school and college. Hopelessness can be intense when certainty of failure is combined with high importance of achievement—if your career depends on not failing an entry exam but you have lost all hope to succeed, you may feel hopeless. Fortunately, full subjective certainty of upcoming failure is relatively rare, and true hopelessness occurs less frequently than less extreme negative emotions, such as moderate anxiety or boredom.

Retrospective outcome emotions include positive emotions such as joy and negative emotions such as frustration and sadness, which do not require much appraisal, except for evaluating one's achievement as good versus poor. More complex retrospective emotions, however, do require more elaborate cognitive judgment. Relief can be triggered when negative expectations are not fulfilled, such as expecting a D on an exam but receiving an A instead. In contrast, disappointment is prompted when the expectation was positive but the outcome is negative. As such, both relief and disappointment are counterfactual emotions that are triggered when a prior expectation has not been fulfilled.

However, there also is a second type of relief—the type of relief one feels when a painful state ends.[7] Both types of relief occur frequently in academia. After an exam, students can feel relief when they receive feedback that is better than expected. Alternatively, they can feel relief because the exam was stressful and is over now. It seems likely that both types of relief serve important functions to ease students' recovery from exam stress, thus also helping their immune system and physical health. Likely, students who are suffering from chronic achievement stress and cannot experience relief are in danger of developing health problems. Research on this important function of students' relief, however, is lacking to date.

Finally, there also are important retrospective outcome emotions that depend on appraisals of control, such as causal attributions of success and failure outcomes. Research has shown that pride is triggered when students attribute success to their own ability or effort, and that gratitude is prompted when success is attributed to help by others, such as parents, peers, or teachers. Shame is induced when failure is attributed to lack of ability, and anger when failure is attributed to the actions of others, such as use of unfair grading practices in the classroom. All of these emotions also depend on value—the more important success and failure are, the more intense these emotions will be.

Other Types of Emotions

Beyond achievement emotions, what about the role of appraisals for other types of academic emotions, such as epistemic, topic, and social emotions as described in Chapter 1? Whereas research on achievement emotions has generated a solid body of evidence on the function of appraisals, studies on these emotions as experienced by students are a new field. From these studies, there is emerging evidence that these emotions are also influenced by students' appraisals of control and value. For example, recent studies on epistemic emotions have shown that surprise, curiosity, and confusion are amplified when the task is deemed important, and when the student feels out of control over understanding the problem and solving the task, curiosity may be replaced by confusion.

However, appraisals of control and value may not be sufficient to explain epistemic emotions. For these emotions, information-oriented appraisals of novelty and cognitive incongruity are the primary triggers. The majority of research in the broader psychological literature has focused on these appraisals as antecedents to epistemic emotions. Novelty and cognitive incongruity can occur under different conditions. For example, incoming information can be novel or inconsistent relative to an individual's prior knowledge, inconsistent with previously processed information, or counter to an individual's prior beliefs about the nature of knowledge. Furthermore, there can be a discrepancy between current knowledge and what an individual wants to know.

For example, imagine the children's reaction when they were told that Pluto is no longer a planet—they were surprised because this new information was inconsistent with their prior knowledge about Pluto being a planet. This new information was unexpected. You might also experience surprise if you read information that contradicts previously read information. For example, imagine you are interested in finding out more about the causes of climate change. In your search, you find that one expert states that climate change is caused by astronomical circumstances, whereas another expert claims that climate change is human-induced. Under this condition, you may be surprised by the incongruity between the information you just read compared to the information you read minutes before. With this example, you may also experience surprise because you believe that experts have reached consensus on the causes of climate change. Being presented with two contrasting expert opinions may be counter to your own personal beliefs about the firm status of knowledge about climate change.

As such, the extent of the surprise you experience may depend on how discrepant the incoming information is compared to prior knowledge, information, and beliefs. In contrast, curiosity arises from an incongruity—or information gap— between what an individual knows and what an individual wants to know, and confusion is triggered from appraisals of uncertainty stemming from unresolved incongruity.

Typically, when new or discrepant information is detected, surprise is the first emotion that occurs. Attention then shifts to the new information, and the autonomic nervous system is aroused. The intensity of surprise that individuals experience depends on their perception of how much cognitive work it will take to explain the surprising event. That is, some surprises are more surprising than others because they are more difficult to explain. In the context of learning, when the intensity of surprise is low (low novelty, low incongruity), learners will typically continue to engage in learning without changing their course of action. If the intensity of surprise is high (high novelty, high incongruity), curiosity may be triggered if the individual has sufficient prior knowledge about the topic or has the skills to understand the information and resolve the discrepancy. However, if novelty and incongruity are high, but the individual has low to no prior knowledge, or does not have the skills necessary to resolve the discrepancy, then confusion will occur. Additionally, when confusion occurs, learners may be more likely to use effortful learning strategies if they value what they are learning compared to when value is low. If effortful strategies are used and the confusion is resolved, individuals are likely to experience joy and possibly relief. However, if confusion cannot be resolved, despite efforts or due to lack of skills, individuals may subsequently experience anxiety and frustration, or boredom if value is low.

Automatization of Appraisals

It is important to note that academic emotions are not always mediated by conscious appraisals of control, value, novelty, or cognitive incongruity. Rather, recurring appraisal-based induction of emotions can become automatic and non-reflective over time. When specific emotion-inducing academic experiences are repeatedly encountered, appraisals and the induction of emotions can become routinized such that conscious mediation of emotions is reduced or no longer occurs.[8] In this way, a direct link can exist between a perceived situation and an emotion (e.g., the mere smell of the chemistry building inducing joy, or anxiety in a student upon entering the classroom after repeated experiences of failure and shame in this room). Such non-reflective, habitual emotions that are not generated by conscious appraisals are quite typical for everyday emotional life. Whenever the situation changes, however, appraisals come into play again, and changes of appraisals can change these emotions. Changing habitual emotions by breaking up situation-emotion contingencies is critical for any kind of educational intervention wanting to change emotions.[9]

The Role of Gender and Achievement Goals

Appraisals function as proximal, immediate causes of emotion. By implication, any individual factors that influence students' appraisals can also influence their emotions (see Figure 3.1). Researchers have focused on two such factors: students' gender and their **achievement goals**.

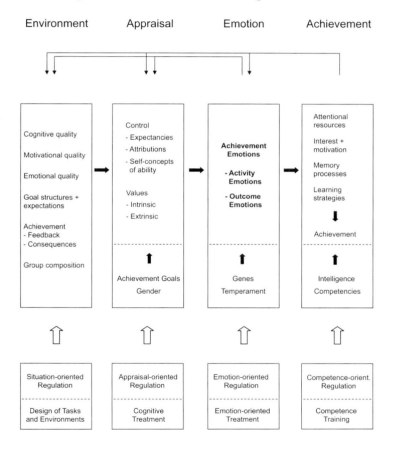

Figure 3.1 Origins, outcomes, and regulation of achievement emotions: Summary of propositions from R. Pekrun's control-value theory[2]

Gender

The influence of students' gender on their emotions has primarily been examined in relation to students' emotions in mathematics. The evidence shows that female students report higher levels of negative emotions in this domain, such as math anxiety, shame, and hopelessness, compared with boys. They also report lower positive emotions, such as enjoyment of math.[10] This stands in stark contrast to the often negligible gender differences in students' performance in mathematics—typically, grades and test scores in mathematics do not differ much between the genders.

Why are girls more afraid of math than boys, and why do they enjoy math less? Gender-linked appraisals provide an answer. Girls and boys do not only differ in their math emotions; they also differ in their self-appraisals in mathematics. Specifically, even if average performance is similar, female students report lower self-perceived ability in mathematics. This difference in perceived competence provides an explanation for the differences in emotions.[10] Together, female students' doubts in their competence and lack of enjoyment in math contribute to their lack of interest in the science, technology, engineering, and math (STEM) subjects and related career decisions, which partly explains the current underrepresentation of females in many STEM-related occupations that involve mathematics as a major component.

However, a few words of caution are in order. First, although these gender differences in math emotions and math perceived competence were observed across countries and in many studies, they are typically small and only describe the average student—they hold for the mean in the population but may not describe the single student. Within any given group of students, the variation of emotions among girls, and among boys, may be much larger than the differences between girls and boys, as noted in Chapter 1. Second, the observed gender differences do not follow a simple plus-minus pattern—there are exceptions to the rule that female students report more negative and less positive emotions in mathematics. Specifically, whereas girls typically report more anxiety, shame, and hopelessness, boys have sometimes been found to report higher levels of anger and boredom than girls in math.[11] Finally, it may even be the case that girls *report* different levels of emotions but do not differ much from boys in the emotions they actually *experience*. Similar to gender differences in actual emotions, differences in self-report may also be due to differences in self-beliefs—if you believe you are not capable of solving math problems, you would also not believe you enjoy working on such problems.[12]

Achievement Goals

Students' achievement goals relate to the successes they want to achieve and the failures they want to avoid. These goals can be organized based on two criteria: the standards used to define achievement and the value of achievement. In terms of standards, researchers distinguish between *mastery* defined by absolute or individual standards and *performance* defined by normative standards. To explain, **absolute standards**—also called criterion-referenced standards—define achievement relative to mastery of the material; **individual standards** define achievement relative to individual improvement and increase of competencies over time; **normative standards** define achievement relative to others (e.g., grading on the curve). For example, one student aims to master learning materials and improve her competencies, whereas another student aims to do well relative to other students. In terms of value, students may aim to approach success (positive value) or to avoid failure (negative value), thus leading to a distinction between *approach* and *avoidance* goals. Combining the two distinctions leads to a taxonomy of four types of achievement goals: **mastery-approach**, **mastery-avoidance**, **performance-approach**, and **performance-avoidance** goals.[13]

Important for the instigation of emotions, achievement goals are assumed to direct and focus attention during the appraisal process.[14] Mastery goals should focus attention on an ongoing activity and its usefulness for competence development. Specifically, mastery-approach goals should focus attention on the controllability and positive value of achievement activities. Therefore, they should foster positive activity emotions like enjoyment of learning and should reduce negative activity emotions such as boredom and anger. In contrast, performance goals should focus attention on normative outcomes (i.e., performance relative to others), thus promoting outcome emotions. Specifically, performance-approach goals focus attention on the controllability and positive value of normative success. Therefore, these goals facilitate prospective hope and retrospective pride (in the case of success). Performance-avoidance goals should focus attention on the uncontrollability and negative value of normative failure. Therefore, these goals promote the experience of prospective anxiety and hopelessness, and of retrospective shame (in the case of failure).

The research evidence supports these hypotheses.[14–16] Best documented are the relations between mastery-approach goals and students' enjoyment of learning, and between performance-avoidance goals and their anxiety. However, recent research also shows clear relationships between goals and other emotions, including negative links between mastery-approach goals and boredom as well as positive links between performance-approach goals and hope and pride, and between performance-avoidance goals and shame and hopelessness. Moreover, it follows from the close relationships between achievement goals and emotions that emotions contribute to the impact of achievement goals on performance: Achievement goals influence students' emotions, and these emotions influence students' learning and achievement as explained in Chapter 2.[17]

However, in interpreting the links between goals and emotions, it is important to note that emotions can reciprocally influence students' goals, such that goals and emotions are linked by reciprocal effects over time. For example, mastery-approach goals promote students' enjoyment of learning, and enjoyment facilitates the adoption of mastery goals. Similarly, performance-avoidance goals prompt anxiety, and anxiety contributes to the adoption of performance-avoidance goals. As such, goals and emotions can be linked in virtuous (approach-oriented) and vicious (avoidance-oriented) cycles, similar to the virtuous and vicious cycles linking emotions and achievement as discussed in Chapter 2.

EMOTION REGULATION AND EMOTIONAL COMPETENCIES

Negative emotions such as anxiety or boredom make us suffer. Alternatively, we can also suffer from a lack of positive emotions. Accordingly, we may want to reduce our negative emotions and increase our positive emotions—a process called **emotion regulation**. Emotion regulation aims to influence the intensity, duration, and type of emotion experienced.[18] It allows the individual to respond in flexible ways to situational demands while taking account of short-term and long-term goals and concerns. In the context of the classroom, successful emotion regulation involves students' capacity to use their emotions as a source of energy yet modify aspects of the emotional experience when it interferes with the pursuit of important goals. In contrast, inability to temper the intensity and duration of one's emotional arousal in the classroom hinders not only learning but social functioning as well. Having access to adequate emotion regulation strategies helps students to feel self-efficacious and to view the learning process as constructive and the classroom environment as supportive. As such, emotion regulation is based on individual competencies to manage and use one's emotions. **Emotional intelligence** is a summary term often used to denote these competencies. In this section, we address emotion regulation and related emotional competencies.

Emotion Regulation

Research has indicated that emotions can be regulated in a variety of ways. We will use the distinction of problem-focused versus emotion-focused coping as well as a process model of emotion regulation to describe different strategies to regulate emotions.

Emotion-Focused Versus Problem-Focused Coping

The term **coping** is used to describe attempts to deal with stress, such as the stress produced by exams and negative emotions. Coping researchers have distinguished between problem-focused strategies of coping that involve attempts to alter a stressor and emotion-focused strategies that attempt to directly change the emotion.[3] Examples of problem-focused coping in educational settings include working hard, seeking help, and making educational career decisions that match one's profile of abilities and interests. Examples of emotion-focused coping include reappraisal (i.e., re-interpreting the situation), self-talk, humor, distraction, relaxation, wishful thinking, self-blame, acting up, distancing, suppression, withdrawal, and self-handicapping.[19]

Depending on the situation, strategies from both categories can be helpful to cope with negative emotions. For example, working hard to prepare for an exam may be helpful if preparation is not yet sufficient; if preparation is good but the student still is fearful of failing the exam, she could reappraise the situation by making clear to herself that she is well prepared and that there may be second chances to re-take the exam even if she would fail despite good preparation. However, in both categories, many of the strategies also can have negative side effects that need to be considered. For example, working hard for too many hours can involve costs for family life and friendships; reappraisal may be detrimental if it is not grounded in reality, such as believing in good chances to succeed when preparation is in fact not sufficient; and using alcohol or medical drugs to fight exam anxiety can have negative effects on physical health.

Selecting a coping strategy is not a one-shot process. In stressful situations, students may experience an urgent need to feel better right away, even though they may also have the intention to resolve the problem. This goal ambivalence will be reflected in the coping strategies that are used. For example, M. Boekaerts reported that students who experienced intense stress in relation to interpersonal stressors, such as being called names by peers, used a double-focused coping strategy.[20] The students realized that it is important to use problem-focused coping (e.g., confronting the aggressor), yet they felt a desire to opt out of the situation to protect their egos (walking away, mental distraction). In other words, problem-oriented and emotion-oriented regulatory goals competed for dominance in the coping process.

Process Model of Emotion Regulation

J. Gross proposed a process model of emotion regulation that provides a more fine-grained account of emotion regulation by highlighting its time course.[18] The model is based on a sequence of processes that are involved in an emotion episode (situation, attention, appraisal, and emotional response). Each of these processes is a potential target for emotion regulation. Gross identified different families of regulation strategies targeting these processes, including situation selection, situation modification, attention deployment, appraisal-oriented cognitive change, and emotion-oriented response modulation (i.e., changing emotional responses such as facial expression). As argued in Pekrun's control-value theory, it is important to additionally consider personal competencies as a target for emotion regulation—enhancing one's competencies can facilitate positive emotions and reduce negative emotions at school (Figure 3.1).[2] As such, we consider five broad categories of emotion regulation: situation-oriented (selection and modification of situations), competence-oriented, attention-oriented, appraisal-oriented, and emotion-oriented regulation. The first four of these categories apply before the full-blown emotional response occurs, which can make these strategies especially adaptive.

(1) Situation-Oriented Regulation

This group of strategies includes situation selection and situation modification. **Situation selection** involves choosing situations that minimize the risk to be confronted with an emotional stressor (e.g., failure, threat, loss) and to maximize the chances to strengthen one's positive emotions. In education, situation selection includes decisions about schools and classes to attend as well as decisions about single learning tasks. In the classroom, students may not always be able to select learning situations. Yet, if they understand what the antecedents of their emotions are, they may try to organize their learning in such a way that they have the best chances for mastery and protect their ego at the same time. For example, if teachers allow their students to decide on different types of instruction (e.g., teacher-regulated learning vs. self-regulated learning) or different task assignment (e.g., easy versus difficult exercises), students can make choices that promote their adaptive emotions.

Situation modification involves efforts to intervene in the physical, social, and instructional environment so as to change its emotional impact. Situation modification is an important strategy in the classroom because it may allow students to solicit social and instructional support. For example, a student may ask her teacher to change the seating arrangement so that she sits next to a friendlier peer, or to supply extra exercises that will allow her to practice deficient skills. Another example is dealing with boredom by asking the teacher to provide more interesting tasks or by chatting with classmates rather than listening to the teacher, called "behavioral approach coping" and "avoidance coping," respectively, by T. Goetz and colleagues.[21] Designing tasks and learning environments in emotionally adaptive ways falls into this category of regulation strategies.

Students need emotional competencies, such as knowledge about the causes for their emotions, to appropriately select and modify situations. Lack of such knowledge is one barrier to effective selection and modification. Another barrier is adequately weighing short-term benefits of situation selection versus longer-term costs. For example, students may feel better if they can postpone a difficult situation (e.g., preparing for a test) and abandon strategies that take effort, and they may be ignorant that such short-term benefits come at the cost of failing an exam.

(2) Competence-Oriented Regulation

In addition to selecting and changing situations in emotionally adaptive ways, changing oneself is an equally important way to regulate emotions. In the academic domain, an especially important strategy is to increase one's cognitive competencies to master academic tasks. With higher competencies in terms of subject matter knowledge and study skills, students reduce the risk of failing exams, thus also reducing their anxiety, shame, and hopelessness. At the same time, the mastery of tasks entailed by competence makes it possible to benefit from all the positive emotions that come with success, such as task enjoyment, pride, and sustained curiosity and interest.

(3) Attention-Oriented Regulation

One way to avoid the generation of negative emotions is to simply ignore stimuli that could trigger these emotions, such as not listening when the teacher provides details about an upcoming exam. Obviously, while alleviating immediate anxiety, such a strategy can have negative long-term effects. Alternatively, paying attention to positive aspects of an academic situation can facilitate the experience of positive emotions, such as focusing on the presence of classmates who are friends.

(4) Appraisal-Oriented Regulation

Emotions can be changed by changing one's appraisals, a process called **reappraisal**. Reappraisal refers to modifying one's interpretation of the situation so that it changes its emotional impact. Reappraisal can pertain to perceptions of control and value that function as immediate causes of emotions, as discussed earlier in this chapter; to situational conditions; and to the emotional response itself. In terms of control, reappraisal can involve changing perception of one's competence and chances to succeed (e.g., "Given the amount of time I invested, I should be able to succeed on the exam"; "I was able to stand my ground last time, so why would I not be able to do it this time?") as well as attributions of success and failure ("Maybe I don't lack the ability, but it's just that I underestimated the amount of preparation needed"). In terms of value, reappraisal involves changing perceptions of the significance of the situation, thus reducing perceived importance and all the negative emotions that are exacerbated when achievement is excessively important ("Is this exam really all that important?").

Alternatively, reappraisal can involve changing situational perceptions. For example, students can note that it is emotionally more helpful to consider errors as opportunities to learn rather than as indicators of lack of ability. Finally, once an emotion has been triggered, reappraisal can also be used to reinterpret the emotion and its component processes. For example, J. Gross and O. John described how athletes and musical performers interpret their physiological arousal prior to going on stage.[22] Some performers interpreted the arousal as stage fright, which may have a debilitating effect, whereas others viewed it as getting pumped up, which may have a performance-enhancing effect. In the academic domain, researchers have demonstrated how students can interpret their anxiety as excitement that benefits learning and how such a reappraisal can both reduce subsequent anxiety and boost performance.[23,24] Generally, empirical research has confirmed that reappraisal is a powerful way to fight negative emotions and up-regulate positive emotions.

(5) Emotion-Oriented Regulation

Emotions can be regulated by influencing the psychological, physiological, and behavioral responses that are part of emotion. Such **response modulation** occurs late in the emotion episode, after response tendencies have been initiated. For example, students who experience tension and bodily symptoms before taking an important test may try to tone down the physiological aspects of anxiety (e.g., increased heart rate, trembling hands) and its psychological symptoms (e.g., worry, feelings of uncertainty) by taking drugs, smoking, drinking, or practicing relaxation techniques.

Expressive suppression is a response-focused strategy that aims to prevent the emotional response from being observed. J. Gross and R. Thompson reported that instructions to suppress one's emotions while viewing emotion-arousing videos successfully decreased expressive behavior but increased rather than decreased sympathetic physiological arousal.[25] Suppression requires continuous monitoring, which taxes cognitive resources. Students who were requested to control their emotions gave up faster on a successive task than those who were not requested to do so—suppression can impede task engagement and persistence.[26] Compared with reappraisal, habitual use of suppression is linked to less positive affect, reduced interpersonal functioning, and lower well-being.[18] Rather than hiding emotions, students may express them verbally or non-verbally. The advantage of emotion expression is that attention is called to what one feels, which may contribute to modifying the situation by changing the behavior of others. For example, peers may become more mindful to what a student feels when he shows his disappointment.

Explicit Versus Implicit Emotion Regulation

A psychological process is called "explicit" when it is conscious, amenable to reflection, and intentionally initiated and surveilled by the individual. When the process does not require conscious attention and deliberate intentions but rather runs automatically, it is called "implicit." **Explicit emotion regulation** requires conscious effort for initiation, demands monitoring during implementation, and is associated with some level of insight and awareness, whereas **implicit emotion regulation** is evoked automatically by the stimulus itself, runs to completion without monitoring, and can happen without insight and awareness.[27] The strategies people use to regulate their emotions vary in explicitness over time and across situations. For example, a student who gets upset when the physics teacher makes a cynical remark about his performance may remind himself that on Mondays the teacher resents coming to work. This reappraisal may automatically reduce his irritation on Mondays. Through repeated use, explicit if-then implementation plans for emotion regulation strategies become habitual, involuntary responses that are used with little awareness, similar to the routinization of cognitive appraisals described earlier.

It is the interplay between explicit and implicit processing that makes emotion regulation adaptive.[25] Explicit emotion regulation can successfully change emotional responses, but it requires extensive cognitive monitoring and hence uses considerable resources in terms of effort and attention. When working on difficult tasks, explicit emotion regulation and task-related information processing may compete for the same limited processing resources. Specifically, down-regulating negative emotions requires resources that may be depleted when the emotions to be regulated are frequent and intense. By contrast, implicit regulation involves less load and is often more reliable. As such, an important goal for educators is to help students develop strategies to reduce excessive negative emotions and promote positive emotions in habitualized and effective ways.

Emotion Regulation Through Psychotherapy

Emotions can be regulated by the individual, but they can also be regulated by others. Teachers and parents can influence students' emotions by designing tasks and learning environments in emotionally appropriate ways, as described in the section on the impact of tasks and environments. However, sometimes the help of therapists is needed. Specifically, psychotherapy can help with reducing excessive negative emotions. This has been intensively researched for students' test anxiety. Individual test anxiety is treatable; in fact, some of the treatments for test anxiety are among the most successful psychological therapies available. Similar to the different individual strategies of emotion regulation, different test anxiety treatments focus on various manifestations and antecedents of this emotion (Figure 3.1). These include affective-physiological symptoms (emotion-oriented therapy), cognitive appraisals (cognitive therapy), and competence deficits caused by lack of strategies for learning and problem solving (skills training, competence development).[9]

Emotion-oriented therapy includes anxiety induction (e.g., flooding), biofeedback procedures, relaxation techniques (e.g., progressive muscle relaxation), and systematic desensitization.[9] **Cognitive therapies** aim to modify anxiety-inducing control beliefs, values, and styles of self-related thinking. Examples are **attributional retraining**, cognitive-attentional training, cognitive restructuring therapy, and stress-inoculation training.[9] **Study-skills training** teaches students to understand and use task-oriented learning strategies and problem-solving skills that promote academic success and thus decrease anxiety. Finally, **multimodal therapies** integrate different procedures to address different symptoms and antecedents of anxiety within one treatment.

Cognitive and multimodal therapies have proven especially effective at both reducing test anxiety and enhancing academic performance. Study-skills training has been shown to successfully reduce test anxiety in students with deficits in their learning strategies. Consistent with the arguments above, therapy focusing exclusively on emotion-oriented procedures has been shown to successfully reduce anxiety but has proven less effective at improving academic achievement. These kinds of therapy address the affective and physiological components of anxiety but not the underlying cognitive components of anxiety that are primarily responsible for the performance-debilitating effects of this emotion.

Emotional Competencies and Emotional Intelligence

The arousal and regulation of emotions depends on the joint action of situational factors and individual competencies. Emotional competencies include abilities to generate, recognize, evaluate, increase or decrease, and make use of one's own emotions. In addition, abilities to recognize and manage other's emotions are important. Relevant for these competencies are factors such as neurophysiological processes involved in the decoding of emotional stimuli and the control of one's emotions; motivational competencies to initiate and perform regulatory actions; as well as cognitive abilities to process emotion-relevant information. As such, a broad variety of abilities, both cognitive and non-cognitive, comprise an individual's emotional competencies.

Despite the diversity of these abilities, the term "emotional intelligence" is often used to denote all of the competencies to generate and regulate emotions.[28] Obviously, this may imply an over-inclusive use of the term "intelligence," as this term is commonly used to denote cognitive abilities (e.g., abilities to think) rather than non-cognitive abilities (e.g., abilities to persist when performing a task). Further adding to the ambiguity of the concept, authors such as D. Goleman and R. Bar-On, who made "emotional intelligence" a popular topic in the 1990s, used the term to denote an even broader array of individual dispositions, including various kinds of personality variables that can directly or indirectly relate to an individual's emotional agency ([29,30]; for a detailed critique, see [31]). For example, Bar-On's concept of emotional intelligence includes, among others, emotional self-awareness, assertiveness, self-regard, self-actualization, independence, empathy, social responsibility, problem solving, reality testing, flexibility, happiness, and optimism. Conceptions of this kind seem more similar to concepts of personality than to a circumscribed set of competencies related specifically to emotion.

Using the term "emotional intelligence" for *cognitive* abilities to recognize, manage, and use emotions—as proposed by

J. Mayer, P. Salovey, and D. Caruso—may invoke fewer misunderstandings.[32] In their model of emotional intelligence, these authors proposed four sets of cognitive abilities: (1) *emotional perception and identification* related to abilities for encoding emotional information, such as being able to recognize emotion from facial expression; (2) *emotional facilitation of thought* involving abilities to use one's own emotions for thinking and cognitive problem solving, such as using a fearful affective state to do simple routine tasks and a joyful mood to be creative; (3) *emotional understanding* related to the evaluation of emotional information, such as students' understanding of why their appraisals of an upcoming exam make them fearful; and (4) *emotion management* involving abilities to regulate one's own emotions and the emotions of others. The focus of this model is on cognitive abilities, thus justifying use of the term "intelligence." In line with the ability-oriented nature of the conception, the authors developed a test measuring the proposed sets of abilities, the current version being the Mayer-Salovey-Caruso Emotional Intelligence Test (MSCEIT).[33]

Given that emotions affect students' academic performance as outlined in Chapter 2, and that the regulation of emotions depends on emotional competencies, measures such as the MSCEIT should predict academic achievement over and above IQ (i.e., scores from traditional intelligence tests) or prior achievement. In fact, some proponents of emotional intelligence, such as D. Goleman, have stated that emotional intelligence should be as, or even more, important for academic achievement than general cognitive abilities.[29] However, to date, research testing this proposition is quite limited and has failed to demonstrate a clear link between emotional intelligence and students' achievement. While some studies found a positive, though weak, association between these variables (e.g., [34,35]), others found null relations, in particular when also including general cognitive abilities as predictors (e.g., [36,37]). Thus, it remains open to question to what extent current measures of emotional intelligence possess explanatory power over and above general IQ.

However, in interpreting this evidence, it has to be taken into account that this is a nascent field of research. It is quite difficult to develop adequate measures of emotional intelligence, and it would be premature to conclude that emotional intelligence is irrelevant for academic achievement. Rather, it remains a challenge for future research to demonstrate how students' emotional intelligence, and their emotion-related competencies more generally, affect learning and performance.

THE INFLUENCE OF TASKS AND LEARNING ENVIRONMENTS

Classroom instruction, the environment in the family, and relationships with peers are likely critically important for the development of students' emotions. However, in contrast to the rich number of studies on the functions of emotions for learning, the impact of task design and learning environments on students' emotions is still largely unexplored. In this field as well, the only major exception is research on test anxiety.[1,9] Lack of structure and clarity in classroom instruction and exams, as well as excessively high task demands, relate positively to students' test anxiety. These effects can be explained when considering the appraisal antecedents of anxiety: lack of perceived control combined with high perceived importance, as discussed earlier. Lack of clarity and high task demands undermine students' sense of competence and control, thus inducing expectancy of failure and prompting anxiety. For example, if teachers do not provide sufficient information about the format, timing, and grading of exams, students' anxiety can be exacerbated.

Furthermore, the format of tasks has been found to be relevant.[9] Open-ended formats (e.g., essay questions) seem to induce more anxiety than multiple-choice formats, likely due to higher demands on attention that are difficult to meet when attentional capacity is used for worrying about failure. In contrast, giving individuals the choice between tasks, relaxing time constraints, and giving second chances in terms of retaking tests has been found to reduce test anxiety, presumably because perceived control is enhanced under these conditions. These findings are in line with research demonstrating that task structures that function to promote autonomy and a sense of control are positively related to intrinsic motivation, cognitive flexibility, positive affect, and well-being.[38]

Regarding social environments, high achievement expectancies from important others, negative feedback after performance, and negative consequences of poor performance (e.g., public humiliation) show moderate to strong positive relations with students' test anxiety.[1,9] Also, competition in classrooms is positively related to students' anxiety, presumably because competition reduces expectancies for success and increases the importance of avoiding failure.[39]

In contrast, researchers found that social support from parents and teachers and a cooperative classroom climate were not related to students' test anxiety scores.[40] This is a surprising finding that needs an explanation. One possibility is that support and anxiety are linked by negative feedback loops. These feedback loops are defined by reciprocal effects of variable A affecting variable B and vice versa, with one of the two effects being positive and the other effect negative. From this perspective, social support can alleviate anxiety (negative effect of support on anxiety), but anxiety can provoke support in the first place (positive effect of anxiety on support), thus yielding an overall zero relation. A second possibility is that some attempts by parents and teachers to support students may be interpreted by students as coercive behavior that conveys high expectations and reduces their autonomy, thus increasing their anxiety.

Factors such as the quality of tasks, expectations from significant others, and the functional importance of achievement likely influence academic emotions other than anxiety as well. The following features of tasks and learning environments likely are relevant for a broad variety of academic emotions (see Figure 3.1).

Cognitive Quality

The cognitive quality of classroom instruction and tasks as defined by their structure, clarity, and potential for cognitive stimulation likely has a positive influence on perceived competence and the perceived value of tasks,[41] thus positively influencing students' emotions. When teachers provide clear explanations and well-structured examples, students can enjoy learning. For epistemic emotions such as surprise and curiosity, tasks that induce appropriate levels of cognitive incongruity may be especially important. An example is contradictory texts on controversial scientific or political issues, such as the causes of climate change or the economic prospects and pitfalls of the UK leaving the European Union.[42]

In addition to structure, clarity, and stimulation, the relative difficulty of tasks is critically important. Task difficulty impacts the likelihood of successful task performance, thus influencing perceived control over task performance and all of the emotions that depend on perceived control as discussed earlier. For example, if the very first questions on an exam are very difficult and cannot be answered, perceived control can decrease to the extent that a student starts to panic or even resigns and does not complete the exam. However, it is not only the level of difficulty as such that is important. Rather, the match between task demands and the student's competencies is important as well. If demands slightly exceed current competencies, the task can be perceived as a challenge that can be enjoyable. In contrast, if the demands are too high (over-challenge) or too low (under-challenge), the incentive value of a task may be reduced to the extent that boredom is experienced, as discussed earlier.[6]

Motivational Quality

Teachers, parents, and peers deliver both direct and indirect messages conveying information about the controllability and motivational value of academic tasks, thus influencing students' emotions. In terms of direct communication, they can influence perceptions of control as well as perceptions of value. For example, perceived control can be influenced by attributing a student's achievement to specific causes. By informing students that their failures are due to lack of ability, they can reduce the students' sense of control and prompt shame and anxiety; in contrast, by attributing failure to lack of effort or study strategies, they can help students to uphold positive expectations and experience hope and confidence. Similarly, perceived value can be influenced by explaining the relevance of learning materials and educational attainment. However, increasing perceived importance can boost not only positive emotions but negative emotions as well—as noted earlier, greater value amplifies all types of emotion, both positive and negative (except for boredom). Specifically, reminding students of the importance of successful performance on tests and exams is a double-edged sword—"fear appeals" can exacerbate students' anxiety.[43]

More indirect ways to increase value include use of learning materials that relate to students' existing interests or stimulate the development of new interests. In addition, learning environments that fulfill students' needs for autonomy and social relatedness can help increasing the perceived value of academic learning. As such, if tasks and environments are shaped such that they meet students' needs, positive activity-related emotions should be fostered. For example, learning environments that support cooperation should help students fulfill their needs for social relatedness, thus making working on academic tasks more enjoyable and promoting their academic as well as social engagement. Tasks and environments supporting autonomy can increase perceived control and, by meeting needs for autonomy, the value of related achievement activities.[44] However, the beneficial effects of autonomy support depend on the match between individual competencies and needs for academic autonomy, on the one hand, and the affordances of these environments, on the other. In case of a mismatch, loss of control and negative emotions could result.

Emotional Quality

Emotions need not always be transmitted through cognitive appraisals of control and value—they can be prompted by others in much more immediate ways. Generally, emotions can be directly transmitted to others by means of nonverbal communication. Displays of emotion conveyed by facial, gestural, and postural expression and the prosodic (i.e., non-semantic) features of speech such as pitch, loudness, and timbre of voice provide information about an individual's emotional state.

These signals can be automatically mimicked by others to the extent that the others experience the same emotion—a process called **emotional contagion**.[45] Emotional contagion has been studied in research on psychotherapy and early mother-child interaction, but it has not yet gained sufficient attention in educational research. It seems very likely that emotional contagion plays a major role in daily classroom interaction, with emotions being transmitted from teachers to students, from students to teachers, and among classmates.

Through emotional contagion, teachers can directly influence the mood in the class. The requirement for contagion is that teachers display rather than suppress their emotions. In fact, a few studies suggest that teachers' enjoyment can strongly facilitate students' enjoyment of class and that this process is mediated through teachers' displayed enthusiasm for teaching.[46] In addition to prompting immediate emotional reactions, emotional contagion can involve observational learning: Watching how others enjoy solving a problem demonstrates that problem solving can be enjoyable, and this observed enjoyment can be adopted by the student. As such, teachers' and classmates' enthusiasm in dealing with tasks can facilitate students' adoption of positive emotions and development of positive academic values.

Goal Structures and Social Expectations

Different standards for defining achievement can imply individualistic (mastery), competitive (normative performance), or cooperative goal structures.[47] **Individualistic goal structures** are conceptually equivalent to mastery goals as described earlier. In these structures, achievement is based on absolute or individual standards. Importantly, in these structures, the achievement of any individual student is independent from the achievement of other students. In contrast, **competitive goal structures** are equivalent to performance goals and based on normative standards, which define a student's achievement relative to the achievement of other students. Under such a definition, individual achievement is dependent on the achievement of others. More precisely, it is a negative function of the achievement of others—the poorer the achievement of others, the better is my own achievement, all other things being equal. Not everybody can succeed in terms of outperforming others, and the (normative) success of some students comes at the cost of failure for others. Finally, in **cooperative goal structures**, individual achievement is a positive function of the achievement of others—the better the contributions of each student, the better the achievement of the whole group.

When these goal structures are provided in academic settings, they conceivably influence emotions in two ways. First, to the extent that these structures are adopted, they influence students' individual achievement goals and any emotions mediated by these goals as outlined earlier. Second, goal structures determine relative opportunities for experiencing success and perceiving control, thus influencing control-dependent emotions. Specifically, competitive goal structures imply, by definition, that some individuals have to experience failure, thus inducing negative outcome emotions such as anxiety and hopelessness in these individuals.

Similarly, the demands implied by an important other's unrealistic expectancies for achievement can lead to negative emotions resulting from reduced subjective control. For example, if parents hold overly high aspirations for their children's academic success, they can reduce children's sense of control to meet their parents' expectations, which can prompt anxiety and ultimately prevent the very attainment that parents had hoped for in the first place.[48]

Feedback and Consequences of Achievement

Cumulative success can strengthen perceived control, and cumulative failure can undermine control. In environments involving frequent assessments, performance feedback is of primary importance for the arousal of academic emotions. In addition, the perceived consequences of success and failure are important, since these consequences affect the instrumental value of achievement outcomes. Positive outcome emotions (e.g., hope for success) can be increased if success produces beneficial long-term outcomes (e.g., future career opportunities), provided sufficient contingency between one's own efforts, success, and these outcomes. Negative consequences of failure (e.g., unemployment), on the other hand, may increase achievement-related anxiety and hopelessness.

Group Composition

The ability level of the classroom determines the likelihood of performing well relative to one's classmates. Other things being equal, chances for performing well relative to others are higher when being in a low-ability classroom compared with being in a high-ability classroom. Therefore, students who perform equally well have higher self-perceptions of competence in a low-ability classroom than in a high-ability classroom—being surrounded by high-achieving, gifted peers reduces a student's self-confidence. H. Marsh has proposed to call this effect the **big-fish–little-pond effect**—all other things being equal, it may be preferable to be a "big fish in a little pond" rather than a relatively small fish in a big pond of high achievers.[49] Because negative self-evaluations of competence can trigger negative emotions such as fear of failure, the "big-fish-little-pond effect" of classroom ability level on self-concept can entail similar effects on students' emotions.

Other things being equal, anxiety has in fact been found to be higher in high-ability classrooms than in low-ability classrooms.[50] The negative effects of membership in a high-achieving classroom pose a conundrum for educators. Placing students in high-ability classes provides them with peers who are role models for cognitive development and can provide cognitive stimulation. However, these possible benefits need to be weighed against the psychosocial costs of such a placement, including the risk for a reduction of self-confidence, decrease in positive emotions, and increase in negative emotions such as anxiety.[51]

Technology-Based Versus Traditional Learning Environments

Learning environments that use computer- and internet-based technology are becoming increasingly more important in twenty-first-century education. Examples are online delivery of instruction, such as Massive Open Online Courses (MOOCs) that make it possible to deliver curricular materials to unlimited numbers of students simultaneously; interactive learning programs and games that make it possible to interact with learning materials; artificial tutors that provide learners with guidance and feedback through the learning process; and virtual reality environments that provide possibilities to learn materials and practice skills in realistic ways, such as surgery skills in medical students in a simulated operating room.[52]

One might be tempted to think that these new types of environments are generally more enjoyable for students than traditional classroom instruction. However, this would a misleading conclusion. Rather, the nascent field of research on emotions in these environments shows that it depends on their specific features if they prompt excitement and curiosity, or confusion, anxiety, and boredom.[53,54] In this respect, technology-based environments do not differ from traditional teacher-based instruction—it's the quality of instruction and assessment procedures that matters. The existing studies confirm that students' enjoyment of these environments is closely linked to their perceptions of the quality of the environment.[54] They also show that the emotional effects need not always be positive. For example, in research comparing students' emotions across on-campus and online business and publication administration classes at a North American university, it was found that online students experienced less boredom than on-campus students but also more technology-related anger, anxiety, and helplessness.[55,56]

DEVELOPMENT ACROSS THE SCHOOL YEARS

At the age of two to three years, children are able to express pride and shame when successfully solving tasks or failing to do so. This suggests that they are able to differentiate internal versus external causation of success and failure. During the early elementary school years, they additionally acquire capabilities to distinguish between different types of internal and external causes (such as ability and effort), to develop related causal expectancies and perceptions of control, and to cognitively combine control-related and value-related information.[57] As such, students have developed the cognitive competencies to experience all major types of achievement emotions early in their academic career.

Empirical evidence on the development of these emotions at school is still scarce. Again, test anxiety studies are an exception. These studies have shown that average scores for test anxiety are low at the beginning of elementary school but increase substantially during the elementary school years.[1,9] This development is congruent to the decline of academic self-concepts of ability during this period and is likely due to increasing realism in academic self-perceptions and to the cumulative failure feedback many students receive across the years in schools today. After elementary school, average anxiety scores stabilize and remain at high levels throughout middle school, high school, and college. However, stability at the group level notwithstanding, anxiety can change in individual students. One important source for individual dynamics is the change of reference groups implied by transitions between schools and classrooms. As noted in the last section, other things being equal, the likelihood of poor achievement relative to peers is higher in high-ability classrooms and lower in low-ability classrooms. Therefore, changing from a low-ability to a high-ability classroom can increase anxiety, while the reverse can happen when entering a low-ability classroom.

While anxiety increases in the average student, positive emotions such as enjoyment of learning seem to decrease across the elementary school years.[58] The decrease of enjoyment can continue through the middle school years,[59] which is consistent with the decline of average scores for subject-matter interest and general attitudes toward school.[60–62] Important factors responsible for this development may be an increase of teacher-centered instruction and academic demands in middle school, the competition between academic and non-academic interests in adolescence, and the stronger selectivity of subject-matter interest that is part of adolescent identity formation: In order to develop individual identity, adolescents need to learn how to prioritize some interests over others, which also entails greater selectivity of their academic enjoyments.

CONCLUSIONS

In sum, individual antecedents as well as academic tasks and learning environments shape students' academic emotions and, consequently, any emotion-dependent engagement with learning. Environments, goals, appraisals, and regulatory behavior can induce, prevent, and modulate students' emotions, and they can shape their objects and contents. Depending on individual goals and the learning environment provided, students' academic life can be infused with positive affect and joyful task engagement, or with anxiety, frustration, and boredom. However, the strong impact of appraisals, tasks, and the environment does not imply that basic mechanisms linking students' emotions with these antecedents vary as a function of appraisal and social context. Rather, these mechanisms seem to be pretty stable across contexts.[63] For example, concerning the context provided by different task domains, students' emotions experienced in mathematics, science, and languages differed in mean levels across domains but showed equivalent internal structures and linkages with other variables across domains in recent research with high school students.[64] Similarly, in a cross-cultural comparison of Chinese and German high school students' emotions in math, we found that mean levels of emotions differed between cultures, with Chinese students reporting more achievement-related enjoyment, pride, anxiety, and shame, and less anger in math.[65] However, the functional linkages of these emotions with appraisals and expectations of important others were equivalent across cultures. Most likely, the general functions of individual and social origins for students' emotions are universal across different task domains, learning environments, and cultural contexts.

REFERENCES

1 Zeidner, M. (2014). Anxiety in education. In R. Pekrun & L. Linnenbrink-Garcia (Eds.), *International handbook of emotions in education* (pp. 265–288). New York: Taylor & Francis.

2 Pekrun, R. (2006). The control-value theory of achievement emotions: Assumptions, corollaries, and implications for educational research and practice. *Educational Psychology Review, 18*, 315–341.

3 Lazarus, R. S., & Folkman, S. (1984). *Stress, appraisal, and coping*. New York: Springer.

4 Weiner, B. (1985). An attributional theory of achievement motivation and emotion. *Psychological Review, 92*, 548–573.

5 Skinner, E. A., (1996). A guide to constructs of control. *Journal of Personality and Social Psychology, 71*, 549–570.

6 Pekrun, R., & Perry, R. P. (2014). Control-value theory of achievement emotions. In R. Pekrun & L. Linnenbrink-Garcia (Eds.), *International handbook of emotions in education* (pp. 120–141). New York: Taylor & Francis.

7 Sweeny, K., & Vohs, K. D. (2012). On near misses and completed tasks: The nature of relief. *Psychological Science, 23*, 464–468.

8 Reisenzein, R. (2001). Appraisal processes conceptualized from a schema-theoretic perspective. In K. R. Scherer, A. Schorr, & T. Johnstone (Eds.), *Appraisal processes in emotion* (pp. 187–201). Oxford, UK: Oxford University Press.

9 Zeidner, M. (1998). *Test anxiety: The state of the art*. New York: Plenum.

10 Frenzel, A. C., Pekrun, R., & Goetz, T. (2007). Girls and mathematics—A "hopeless" issue? A control-value approach to gender differences in emotions towards mathematics. *European Journal of Psychology of Education, 22*, 497–514.

11 Pekrun, R., Lichtenfeld, S., Marsh, H. W., Murayama, K., & Goetz, T. (2017). Achievement emotions and academic performance: Longitudinal models of reciprocal effects. *Child Development*. Advance online publication. doi: 10.1111/cdev12704

12   Goetz, T., Bieg, M., Lüdtke, O., Pekrun, R., & Hall, N. C. (2013). Do girls really experience more anxiety in mathematics? *Psychological Science*, 24, 2079–2087.

13   Elliot, A. J., & McGregor, H. (2001). A 2 x 2 achievement goal framework. *Journal of Personality and Social Psychology*, 80, 501–519.

14   Pekrun, R., Elliot, A. J., & Maier, M. A. (2006). Achievement goals and discrete achievement emotions: A theoretical model and prospective test. *Journal of Educational Psychology*, 98, 583–597.

15   Huang, C. (2011). Achievement goals and achievement emotions: A meta-analysis. *Educational Psychology Review*, 23, 359–388.

16   Goetz, T., Sticca, F., Pekrun, R., Murayama, K., & Elliot, A. J. (2016). Intraindividual relations between achievement goals and discrete achievement emotions: An experience sampling approach. *Learning and Instruction*, 41, 115–125.

17   Pekrun, R., Elliot, A. J., & Maier, M. A. (2009). Achievement goals and achievement emotions: Testing a model of their joint relations with academic performance. *Journal of Educational Psychology*, 101, 115–135.

18   Jacobs, S. E., & Gross, J. J. (2014). Emotion regulation in education: Conceptual foundations, current applications, and future directions. In R. Pekrun & L. Linnenbrink-Garcia (Eds.), *International handbook of emotions in education* (pp. 183–201). New York: Taylor & Francis.

19   Boekaerts, M., & Röder, I. (1999). Stress, coping, and adjustment in children with a chronic disease: A review of the literature. *Disability and Rehabilitation*, 21, 311–337.

20   Boekaerts, M. (1999). Coping in context: Goal frustration and goal ambivalence in relation to academic and interpersonal goals. In E. Frydenberg (Ed.). *Learning to cope: Developing as a person in complex societies* (pp. 175–197). Oxford, UK: Oxford University Press.

21   Goetz, T., & Hall, N. C. (2014). Academic boredom. In R. Pekrun & L. Linnenbrink-Garcia, *International handbook of emotions in education* (pp. 311–330). New York: Taylor & Francis.

22   Gross, J. J., & John, O. P. (2002). Wise emotion regulation. In L. F. Barrett & P. Salovey (Eds.), *The wisdom of feelings: Psychological processes in emotional intelligence* (pp. 297–318). New York: Guilford Press.

23   Jamieson, J. P., Mendes, W. B., Blackstock, E., & Schmader, T. (2010). Turning the knots in your stomach into bows: Reappraising arousal improves performance on the GRE. *Journal of Experimental Social Psychology*, 46, 208–212.

24   Brooks, A. W. (2013). Get excited: Reappraising pre-performance anxiety as excitement. *Journal of Experimental Psychology: General, 143,* 1144–1158.

25   Gross, J. J., & Thompson, R. A. (2007). Emotion regulation: Conceptual foundations. In J. J. Gross (Ed.), *Handbook of emotion regulation* (pp. 3–26). New York: Guilford Press.

26   Baumeister, R. F., Zell, A. L., & Tice, D. M. (2007). How emotions facilitate and impair self-regulation. In J. J. Gross (Ed.), *Handbook of emotion regulation* (pp. 408–427). New York: Guilford Press.

27   Gyurak, A., Gross, J. J., and Etkin, A. (2011). Explicit and implicit emotion regulation: A dual-process framework. *Cognition and Emotion, 25,* 400–412.

28   Goetz, T., & Bieg, M. (2016). Academic emotions and their regulation via emotional intelligence. In A. A. Lipnevich, F. Preckel, & R. D. Roberts, *Psychosocial skills and school systems in the 21st century: Theory, research and practice* (pp. 279–298). New York: Springer.

29   Goleman, D. (1995). *Emotional intelligence.* New York: Bantam.

30   Bar-On, R. (1997). *The Emotional Intelligence Inventory (EQ-I): Technical manual.* Toronto, Canada: Multi-Health Systems.

31   Matthews, G., Zeidner, M., & Roberts, R. D. (2002). *Emotional intelligence: Science and myth.* Cambridge, MA: MIT Press.

32   Mayer, J. D., Salovey, P., & Caruso, D. (2000). Emotional intelligence as Zeitgeist, as personality, and as a mental ability. In R. Bar-On & J. D. A. Parker (Eds.), *The handbook of emotional intelligence* (pp. 92–117). San Francisco, CA: Jossey-Bass.

33   Mayer, J. D., Salovey, P., & Caruso, D. (2002). *Mayer-Salovey-Caruso Emotional Intelligence Test (MSCEIT).* Toronto, Ontario, Canada: Multi-Health Systems.

34   Brackett, M. A., Mayer, J. D., & Warner, R. M. (2004). Emotional intelligence and its relation to everyday behaviour. *Personality and Individual Differences, 36,* 1387–1402.

35   Di Fabio, A., & Palazzeschi, L. (2009). An in-depth look at scholastic success: Fluid intelligence, personality traits or emotional intelligence? *Personality and Individual Differences, 46,* 581–585.

36   Amelang, M., & Steinmayr, R. (2006). Is there a validity increment for tests of emotional intelligence in explaining the variance of performance criteria? *Intelligence, 34,* 459–468.

37 Rossen, E., & Kranzler, J. H. (2009). Incremental validity of the Mayer-Salovey-Caruso Emotional Intelligence Test Version 2.0 (MSCEIT) after controlling for personality and intelligence. *Journal of Research in Personality*, 43, 60–65.

38 Deci, E. L., & Ryan, R. M. (1987). The support of autonomy and the control of behavior. *Journal of Personality and Social Psychology*, 53, 1024–1037.

39 Wigfield, A., & Eccles, J. S. (1990). Test anxiety in the school setting. In M. Lewis & S. M. Miller (Eds.), *Handbook of developmental psychopathology: Perspectives in developmental psychology* (pp. 237–250). New York: Plenum Press.

40 Hembree, R. (1988). Correlates, causes, effects, and treatment of test anxiety. *Review of Educational Research*, 58, 47–77.

41 Cordova, D. I., & Lepper, M. R. (1996). Intrinsic motivation and the process of learning: Beneficial effects of contextualization, personalization, and choice. *Journal of Educational Psychology*, 88, 715–730.

42 Muis, K. R., Pekrun, R., Sinatra, G. M., Azevedo, R., Trevors, G., Meier, E., & Heddy, B. (2015). The curious case of climate change: Testing a theoretical model of epistemic beliefs, epistemic emotions, and complex learning. *Learning and Instruction*, 39, 168–183.

43 Putwain, D. W., Remedios, R., & Symes, W. (2015). Fear appeals used prior high-stakes examinations: Why are they appraised as threatening and do they impact on subjective task value? *Learning and Instruction*, 40, 21–28.

44 Tsai, Y.-M., Kunter, M., Lüdtke, O., & Trautwein, U. (2008). What makes lessons interesting? The role of situational and individual factors in three school subjects. *Journal of Educational Psychology*, 100, 460–472.

45 Hatfield, E., Cacioppo, J. T., & Rapson, R. L. (1994). *Emotional contagion.* New York: Cambridge University Press.

46 Frenzel, A. C., Goetz, T., Lüdtke, O., Pekrun, R., & Sutton, R. E. (2009). Emotional transmission in the classroom: Exploring the relationship between teacher and student enjoyment. *Journal of Educational Psychology*, 101, 705–716.

47 Johnson, D. W., & Johnson, R. T. (1974). Instructional goal structure: Cooperative, competitive or individualistic. *Review of Educational Research*, 4, 213–240.

48 Murayama, K., Pekrun, R., Suzuki, M., Marsh, H. W., & Lichtenfeld, S. (2016). Don't aim too high for your kids: Parental over-aspiration

undermines students' learning in mathematics. *Journal of Personality and Social Psychology, 111*, 166-179.

49 Marsh, H. W. (1987). The big-fish-little-pond effect on academic self-concept. *Journal of Educational Psychology, 79*, 280–295.

50 Preckel, F., Zeidner, M., Goetz, T., & Schleyer, E. J. (2008). Female "big fish" swimming against the tide: The "big-fish-little-pond effect" and gender-ratio in special gifted classes. *Contemporary Educational Psychology, 33*, 78–96.

51 Pekrun, R., Murayama, K., Marsh, H. W., Goetz, T., & Frenzel, A. C. (2017). *Class-average achievement undermines students' enjoyment of mathematics.* Manuscript submitted for publication.

52 Calvo, R. A., & D'Mello, S. K. (Eds.). *New perspectives on affect and learning technologies* (Explorations in the learning sciences, instructional systems and performance technologies, Vol. 3). New York: Springer.

53 D'Mello, S. K. (2013). A selective meta-analysis on the relative incidence of discrete affective states during learning with technology. *Journal of Educational Psychology, 105*, 1082–1099.

54 Loderer, K., Pekrun, R., & Lester, J. (2017). *Beyond cold technology: A meta-analysis of emotions in technology-based learning environments.* Manuscript submitted for publication.

55 Butz, N. T., Stupnisky, R. H., & Pekrun, R. (2015). Students' emotions for achievement and technology use in synchronous hybrid graduate programmes: A control-value approach. *Research in Learning Technology, 23*, 1–16. Published online.

56 Butz, N. T., Stupnisky, R. H., Pekrun, R., Jensen, J. L., & Harsell, D. M. (2016). The impact of emotions on student achievement in synchronous hybrid business and public administration programs: A longitudinal test of control-value theory. *Decision Sciences Journal of Innovative Education, 14*, 441–474.

57 Heckhausen, H. (1991). *Motivation and action.* New York: Springer.

58 Helmke, A. (1993). Die Entwicklung der Lernfreude vom Kindergarten bis zur 5. Klassenstufe [Development of enjoyment of learning from kindergarten to grade 5]. *Zeitschrift für Pädagogische Psychologie, 7*, 77–86.

59 Pekrun, R., vom Hofe, R., Blum, W., Frenzel, A. C., Goetz, T., & Wartha, S. (2007). Development of mathematical competencies in adolescence:

The PALMA longitudinal study. In M. Prenzel (Ed.), *Studies on the educational quality of schools* (pp. 17–37). Münster, Germany: Waxmann.

60   Eccles, J. S., & Roeser, R. W. (2009). Schools, academic motivation, and stage-environment fit. In R. M. Lerner & L. Steinberg (Eds.), *Handbook of adolescent psychology* (Vol. 2, pp. 404–434). Hoboken, NJ: Wiley.

61   Wigfield, A., & Cambria, J. (2010). Students' achievement values, goal orientations, and interest: Definitions, development, and relations to achievement outcomes. *Developmental Review*, 30, 1–35.

62   Frenzel, A. C., Goetz, T., Pekrun, R., & Watt, H. M. G. (2010). Development of mathematics interest in adolescence: Influences of gender, family, and school context. *Journal of Research on Adolescence*, 20, 507–537.

63   Pekrun, R. (2009). Global and local perspectives on human affect: Implications of the control-value theory of achievement emotions. In M. Wosnitza, S. A. Karabenick, A. Efklides, & P. Nenniger (Eds.), *Contemporary motivation research: From global to local perspectives* (pp. 97–115). Toronto, Canada: Hogrefe.

64   Goetz, T., Frenzel, A. C., Pekrun, R., Hall, N. C., & Lüdtke, O. (2007). Between- and within-domain relations of students' academic emotions. *Journal of Educational Psychology*, 99, 715–733.

65   Frenzel, A. C., Thrash, T. M., Pekrun, R., & Goetz, T. (2007). Achievement emotions in Germany and China: A cross-cultural validation of the Academic Emotions Questionnaire-Mathematics (AEQ-M). *Journal of Cross-Cultural Psychology*, 38, 302–309.

Four

Teacher Emotions

Learning and teaching is "kind of a rollercoaster. It's periods of brilliant sunshine, warm success, followed by deep valleys of depression and frustration."

(Quote from a teacher interview conducted by
C. Scott and R. Sutton)[1]

Traditionally, research on emotions in education has focused on students' emotions.[2] In this chapter, we provide a different perspective by focusing on teachers. In educational research, teachers have typically been viewed as providers of classroom instruction and learning environments. A substantial amount of research has been dedicated to investigating teaching quality and classroom climates, including classroom goal structures as well as social interaction between teachers and students and among students, as discussed in Chapter 3.[2,3] Less attention has been directed toward teachers themselves—their motives, goals, and affective experiences.[4,5]

One exception to the neglect of teacher affect is the relatively large body of literature on teacher burnout. Compared to other professionals, teachers have a relatively high risk of suffering from burnout.[6] Dropout due to psychological reasons (e.g., depression, exhaustion, or anxiety disorders) is fairly high among teachers. However, most of the literature on burnout adopts a clinical perspective, targeting severe states of emotional exhaustion, reduced personal accomplishment, and depersonalization.[7] In contrast, the present chapter seeks to explore teacher emotions from a broader perspective, and it considers the entire range of positive and negative emotions, from mild to intense states.

We first provide an overview of the frequency of several different emotions that teachers typically experience in the classroom. Next, we discuss related affective constructs addressed in current research on teachers' personality, including teachers' burnout, emotional labor, enthusiasm, and achievement goals. Finally, the chapter provides insight into what is known about possible origins and outcomes of teacher emotions.

TEACHER EMOTIONS: MEASUREMENT AND OCCURRENCE

In the existing literature, three approaches are used to assess teachers' emotions. The first and dominant one is qualitative interview studies. These studies have typically explored teacher emotions by using broadly framed questions regarding how teachers feel about their jobs. Second, researchers have used questionnaire instruments similar to the Achievement Emotions Questionnaire for students described in Chapter 1. An example is the **Teacher Emotions Scales** (TES) developed by A. Frenzel and her colleagues.[8] Finally, teacher emotions have been assessed as they occur in real time, using the experience-sampling method, also referred to as ecological momentary assessment.[9] Experience-sampling studies typically involve repeated assessments of data, usually collected several times a day over a certain period of time (typically one to two weeks), and participants are asked to indicate their emotional state as it is "right now." By implication, the data are assessed in natural settings in the field. Generally, the advantage of experience sampling is that responses are less influenced by participants' ability to correctly recollect experienced emotions.

All three types of approaches typically address specific emotions: Researchers describe teachers' enjoyment or pride, or their anger or anxiety, rather than reporting more generally about their positive or negative affect. Since a key goal of the present chapter is to summarize the existing research on teacher emotions, we present research findings arranged according to these specific emotions, including enjoyment, pride, anger, anxiety, shame/guilt, pity, and boredom. These emotions were selected based on their salience in the literature, indicated by the number of studies that directly addressed these emotions, by their frequency reported in narrative studies, and by the frequency of their actual experience as reported in the studies that used experience-sampling methods. Furthermore, the vast majority of research findings pertains to teachers' emotions during teaching in class, since this is the primary task of a teacher. Considerably less is known about teacher emotions related to preparing for teaching, giving exams, working with parents, or dealing with colleagues and supervisors (even though these activities can also arouse intense emotions). Therefore, the present chapter also focuses on emotions related to teaching.

Positive Emotions

Enjoyment

"*It was such a pleasure to see C's engagement in class today; normally he is a very withdrawn kid*" (quote from a teacher interview conducted by A. Frenzel).[10] As A. Hargreaves emphasized in his writings, teaching offers many emotional rewards.[11] Indeed, enjoyment can be considered one of the most salient emotions experienced by teachers during teaching. Positive emotions, specifically enjoyment, were dominant across studies that used experience sampling to explore the frequency and intensity of teachers' emotions.[4,12,13] This is in line with research conducted in other fields, which highlights the prominence of positive emotions among humans.[14] However, it is possible that teachers exaggerate their experience of enjoyment when being asked about their emotional experiences in class. Unlike other professions, where it might be socially acceptable to admit that work is not always "fun," the teaching profession is credited with very high ideals. Emotionally, teachers may have the expectation that they should always enjoy teaching or love all of their students (see also the section on teachers' "emotional labor").[11]

Pride

"I felt proud when I overcame my tendency to procrastinate on grading and returned my 8th graders' essays on time."[10] Given teachers' role in student education, teachers can experience pride as a result of not only their own but also their students' accomplishments. Pride as a key emotion experienced by teachers was addressed in the 1970s by D. Lortie.[15] In line with this work, pride has been identified as a highly relevant emotion for teachers both in studies exploring teacher emotions through interviews and in studies using experience sampling.[16,17] Overall, pride can be considered the second-most salient positive emotion for teachers, after enjoyment.

Negative Emotions

Anger

"I was really angry at J. today when I again caught her not having done her homework."[10] In studies exploring teacher emotions through experience sampling, anger is identified as the most prominent negative emotion, and this finding is supported by qualitative and narrative research on teachers' emotions.[18,19] Teachers may experience anger toward themselves, such as when they are unsatisfied with how they structured a lesson. More typically, they are angry at their students, like when students are misbehaving. The latter is likely one of the most salient reasons why teachers experience anger (see the section on origins of teacher emotions). However, it is important to note that experiencing and displaying anger is socially undesirable, particularly for teachers.[19] Therefore, teachers' reports of frequency and intensity of anger experienced during teaching might be downwardly biased.

Anxiety

"I get really tense when I feel the students can tell that I am not really prepared for class and basically improvising the lesson design as we go along."[10] A considerable amount of research has been conducted on anxiety in the classroom, with the vast majority of studies focusing on student anxiety and, more specifically, on students' test anxiety (see Chapters 2 and 3). In contrast, little research attention has been directed toward teacher anxiety. Existing reviews on teacher anxiety date back to the 1970s.[20,21] No systematic reviews on teachers' anxieties and concerns have been published since that time. This is astounding given that anxiety is one of the key basic negative emotions that individuals experience. As explained in Chapter 1, anxiety is comprised of aversive affective and physiological experiences (feeling uneasy and nervous, sweating, shaking, etc.) as well as unpleasant thoughts and motivational impulses (such as worries and desires to flee or leave the situation). Anxiety typically occurs when people are confronted with uncertainty and threat, and when they perceive their own potential to cope

with the threat as low (see Chapter 3). Clearly, this is an emotion that is also relevant to teaching. In qualitative interview studies, teachers reported feeling anxious or scared when they were unsatisfied with their own teaching performance and did not perceive themselves as being capable of improving.[16] Feelings of anxiety can also be triggered by lack of preparedness to teach and disciplinary issues in the classroom.[22] Some authors suggest that teaching-related anxiety is particularly pronounced among young teachers and pre-service teachers.[23]

However, the overall frequency and intensity of anxiety reported by teachers is relatively low when judged by studies using experience sampling. One possible explanation is that formal feedback on teaching performance is rarely provided to teachers and that there are fewer and less explicit consequences for teachers' failures in classroom teaching, as compared with students who regularly take formal tests that have important consequences. Therefore, anxiety about poor performance might be lower for teachers than for students—even though this seems to be changing as principles of accountability have entered schools. In the United States, the No Child Left Behind Act (NCLB) federalized an approach that rewarded or punished schools for student test scores in the 1990s. More recently, there has been growing interest in pay for performance plans that reward or punish individual teachers rather than entire schools. Thus, it may become more commonplace that teachers are evaluated based on students' test scores and observer ratings in the classroom and that such evaluations are linked to consequences like contract renewal and merit raises.[24] Teachers' achievement anxiety will likely rise as a result of these developments. However, so far no research has addressed teacher anxiety in response to being evaluated.

One specific form of anxiety that has been addressed in the context of teaching is mathematics anxiety.[21] In many colleges in the United States as well as other countries, the mathematics requirements to qualify for teacher education, specifically at the elementary level, are low. As a result, individuals can successfully pursue a career in teaching even if they tend to dislike math or suffer from math anxiety. Nevertheless, they may later be required to teach mathematics—as is the case with elementary school teachers who typically teach all core subjects. Thus, math anxiety may be a relevant issue for a number of teachers, particularly at the elementary level.[25]

Shame and Guilt

"When I later found out the reason why J. hadn't done her homework, I felt ashamed that I had been so harsh on her."[10] Shame and guilt are among the self-conscious emotions—that is, emotions that involve thoughts about one's own attributes and actions. Laypeople may often use the terms "shame" and "guilt" synonymously. However, emotion researchers argue that they are distinct, with guilt reflecting a negative evaluation of one's behavior and shame reflecting a more global negative evaluation of the self. For example, teachers may experience guilt when they have not prepared their class well for a specific test and students receive low test scores. In contrast, teachers may feel shame when they feel more generally incapable of providing quality instruction in a subject. As many teachers are highly committed to their jobs but may have doubts about their capability and the quality of their teaching, they are also susceptible to intense experiences of shame and guilt. For example, teachers report experiencing feelings of shame or guilt for having betrayed a personal ideal, standard, or commitment.[26]

Shame and guilt are not only self-conscious emotions; they also are social emotions—they are typically tied to the actual or imagined negative judgment of others. The practice of teaching involves having several "spectators"—the students. Thus, the potential threat of being negatively judged by this "audience" is high for teachers. Indeed, teachers have reported feelings of shame and guilt in qualitative interview studies. For example, T. Bibby reported that teachers felt shame as a result of other people's criticism of their lack of knowledge in mathematics.[27] However, findings from studies using experience sampling suggest that shame is not experienced frequently.[28] One possible reason for low frequency is that feelings of shame and guilt simply did not occur during the times sampled in these studies (lesson periods/time at school), because they may be felt only retrospectively, when reflecting about a teaching period, or in the evening when procrastinating preparation of tomorrow's lessons.

Pity

"And I really felt sorry for J. as she cried so hard about having to stay late at school to finish her homework."[10] There are limited references to this emotion in the literature on teacher emotions. Hence, the frequency and intensity of this emotion as experienced by teachers cannot be judged from existing research. However, teachers' pity has been the focus of a few studies addressing the links between emotions and causal attributions.[29] According to this literature, teachers experience pity when students' academic failures are attributed to factors beyond the control of the students, such as their low ability. In contrast, failures attributed to factors within students' control, such as their lack of effort, is likely to trigger anger (see also the section on origins of teacher emotions).

Boredom

In research on emotions at work, boredom has been studied in repetitive, blue-collar jobs, but rarely for white-collar, intellectually demanding jobs such as teaching. In the academic context, boredom has been studied among students (see Chapters 2 and 3) but rarely among teachers. Is it at all conceivable that teachers would feel bored during teaching? While barely any mention of boredom can be found in interviews with teachers, research using experience sampling has revealed that this emotion is clearly relevant to teachers. Specifically, in an experience sampling study by E. Becker, boredom was one of the most prominent negative emotions, with teachers reporting being bored during 26% of classroom instruction time.[17] Thus, it appears that teacher boredom deserves more attention than it has received so far.

RELATED AFFECTIVE AND MOTIVATIONAL CONSTRUCTS

In this section, we discuss four affective-motivational constructs that more broadly relate to emotions and are relevant to teachers. These constructs include teachers' burnout, emotional labor, enthusiasm, and achievement goals, which are popular topics in the current research literature.

Teacher Burnout

Burnout is an affective teacher variable that has received considerable attention by researchers and practitioners alike. Burnout is typically described as a psychological syndrome in response to chronic interpersonal stressors on the job. The multidimensional theory of burnout proposed by C. Maslach and her colleagues continues to be the predominant framework in research on burnout.[6,7] In this framework, the three key dimensions of burnout are emotional exhaustion, feelings of cynicism and detachment from the job, and a sense of lack of professional efficacy.

Even though burnout is clearly an emotional phenomenon and the construct has been studied for decades in relation to teachers, few studies have attempted to analyze the link between teachers' burnout and their emotions. M. Chang argues that experiences of burnout and different emotions during teaching likely have common and overlapping origins (see the section on origins of teacher emotions).[23] It is plausible that burnout is associated with decreased levels of positive emotions (such as enjoyment or pride) and increased levels of negative emotions (such as anger, anxiety, or guilt). In line with this reasoning, A. Frenzel and colleagues found that teachers who reported high levels of emotional exhaustion in their jobs also reported lower levels of enjoyment and elevated levels of anxiety and anger during teaching.[8]

Emotional Labor

"*You never show negative emotions in front of a class. You always display joy and never negative feelings, this would screw up students' ability to learn. Also, it is the job of the teacher to keep cool, even under pressure*" (quote from a teacher diary).[10] **Emotional labor** has been described as the "effort, planning, and control needed to express organizationally desired emotion during interpersonal transactions" ([30] p. 987). The notion of "organizationally desired emotions," also referred to as "emotion rules" or "display rules," implies that the expression of specific emotions (typically positive and pro-social emotions) is expected in certain jobs. As such, these emotions need to be up-regulated. On the other hand, emotions that are not expected (typically negative and anti-social emotions) should not be expressed—that is, they need to be down-regulated on the job. However, it is not always easy to increase positive emotions and to decrease negative emotions. Therefore, the felt emotion and the emotional expression displayed for the sake of complying with emotion rules can diverge. This incongruence between the emotion an individual experiences and the emotion expressed can been referred to as emotional dissonance or inconsistency. For example, contempt for a student and the expression of happiness and friendliness expected from a teacher would not be consistent.

The existence of—at least implicit—emotion rules has been considered in a few studies of teacher emotions. As P. Schutz and his colleagues report, to construct an optimal learning environment, teachers are typically expected to display pleasant emotions and suppress unpleasant emotions in their interactions with students.[31] R. Sutton identified various sources of implicit emotion rules for teachers, including personal role perceptions, family and cultural background, teacher education programs, and fellow teachers. Consistent with this, 29 out of 30 teachers interviewed by Sutton reported effortfully regulating their emotions.[32]

Clearly, emotional labor, emotion rules, and emotional dissonance play a key role for teachers' emotions. Experiencing negative emotions such as anger or anxiety is unpleasant for most individuals. However, in the teaching profession, the strain resulting from experiencing these emotions is intensified because anger and anxiety are expected to be suppressed during classroom instruction and interaction with students. In contrast, positive emotions are expected to be displayed even if they are not experienced, which implies that they need to be faked. Suppressing negative emotions and faking positive emotions constitutes specific work stressors for teachers.[33]

Enthusiasm

Teacher enthusiasm is often considered as one of the key conditions for effective instruction and student motivation. Some researchers refer to enthusiasm as behavior in terms of a motivating, energetic teaching style. In this context, researchers also refer to teacher expressiveness or teacher immediacy.[34] Other researchers conceive of enthusiasm as a subjective experience in terms of the excitement teachers feel toward teaching and toward the subject matter.[35] The latter conceptualization of enthusiasm renders it similar to teaching enjoyment. In fact, in M. Kunter et al.'s studies, teaching enthusiasm was assessed by items such as "I really enjoy teaching."[35] An important finding of these studies is that it is worthwhile to differentiate between teachers' experiences of enthusiasm (or enjoyment) derived from teaching and their enthusiasm (or enjoyment) derived from the subject being taught.

To distinguish between enthusiasm and enjoyment, it is important to conceptually separate behavior (enthusiastic teaching) from the enjoyment experienced when engaging in such behavior.[35,36] Enthusiastic teaching and enjoyment can exist independently from each other within teachers: Some teachers may manage to display an enthusiastic teaching style without really enjoying a lesson; other teachers may actually enjoy teaching but not be able to display their enjoyment in terms of an enthusiastic teaching style. However, it is likely that teacher enthusiasm and enjoyment frequently occur together. Enjoyment manifests in expressive behaviors that are characteristic of an enthusiastic teaching style, including gestures, varied intonation, frequent eye contact, emotive facial expressions, movement while lecturing, and use of humor and lively examples. Existing empirical research clearly shows that teacher enthusiasm as perceived by students, and enjoyment as experienced by teachers, are positively related.[36]

Achievement Goals

As discussed in Chapter 3, goals play a crucial role as individual antecedents of emotions. Drawing on the large body of literature on students' achievement goals, experts have recently begun to acknowledge that teachers' achievement goals may be worthy of exploration as well. R. Butler was among the first to propose that achievement goal theory could provide a useful framework for conceptualizing qualitative differences in teachers' motives for teaching.[37,38] She developed a self-report measure called "goal orientations for teaching," with items reflecting the desire to (a) learn and acquire professional competence (mastery goal), (b) demonstrate superior teaching ability (ability-approach goal), (c) avoid demonstrating inferior teaching ability (ability-avoidance goal), and (d) get through the day with little effort (work-avoidance goal). Studies of these goals show that they are relevant to teachers' instructional practices, interest in teaching, and burnout, and to help-seeking behaviors of both teachers and students.[37,38] More recently, Butler proposed that a fifth type of teacher goal, namely "relational goals," may also play a crucial role.[39] These goals correspond to teachers' aspirations to build close and caring relationships with students. Butler showed that teachers who had strong relational goals provided not only better social support but also more mastery-oriented instruction (e.g., by making an effort to recognize students' individual progress regardless of their achievement relative to the class). Teachers' goals likely are related to their emotions, as is the case with students' goals and emotions (see Chapter 3).

ORIGINS AND EFFECTS OF TEACHER EMOTIONS

In this section, we discuss antecedents and outcomes of teachers' emotions. The discussion is framed according to the reciprocal model of causes and effects of teacher emotions proposed by A. Frenzel and colleagues (see Figure 4.1).[4,13,40] This model is one possible approach to understanding and framing teacher emotions. It addresses teacher emotions specifically from an achievement perspective, where the pursuit of success and happiness, and avoidance of failure and unhappiness, are central processes. As such, this

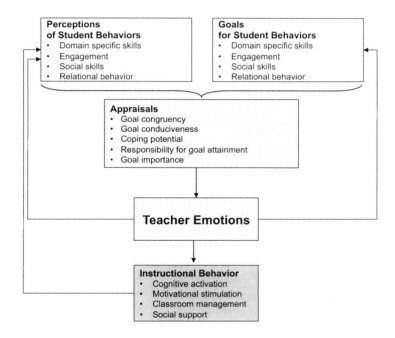

Figure 4.1 Origins and effects of teacher emotions: A. Frenzel's model of reciprocal effects

Adapted from [4]

model addresses emotions that result from teachers' judgments regarding the success or failure of their own teaching efforts, since these are particularly salient for teachers. For example, the model addresses teachers' pride in capturing their students' interest in a new topic given the teachers' engaged introduction of the topic, or teachers' anger if students are inattentive and, as a result, struggle with grasping a topic. However, this model does not address purely social emotions, such as empathy with a suffering child or contempt for a colleague or principal.

The overarching theoretical frameworks that guide the model are appraisal and causal attribution theories. As outlined in Chapter 3, these theories explain that emotions are primarily caused by individuals' judgments about situations and events rather than by the situations and events themselves. Appraisals are cognitive judgments about situations and events, such as whether they are considered benign (positive) or harmful (negative). Causal attributions are one specific type of appraisal. They pertain to the perceived causes for events (who or what has caused an event). Appraisal and attribution theories posit that certain combinations of cognitive judgments lead to specific emotions. For instance, as discussed in Chapter 3, feelings of gratitude are aroused in situations that are perceived as positive and caused by another individual, whereas pride is aroused in situations that are perceived as positive and caused by oneself. Furthermore, Frenzel et al.'s model is based on general psychological insights regarding the effects of human emotions. In applying and elaborating these theoretical ideas specifically to the classroom, Frenzel et al. outline reciprocal relationships between students' classroom behaviors, teacher emotions, and teachers' instructional behaviors.

Origins of Teacher Emotions

Appraisals

Teachers' appraisals of events that occur in the classroom are of primary importance for their emotions (marked in light grey in Figure 4.1). The upper part of Figure 4.1 depicts how these appraisals may be formed (marked in white), and the lower part depicts the suggested effects of teacher emotions on their instructional behavior (marked in dark grey).

More specifically, teachers' emotional experiences are determined by their judgments of whether students' behavior in class is aligned with teachers' classroom goals. At certain time points (continually during instruction, but also at the end of a period, end of an instructional unit, or end of a school year), teachers assess whether or not their set goals were achieved based on their perceptions of the students' behaviors and, as part of this process, cognitively appraise the activities of their classroom. This is in line with D. Lortie's assertion that teachers experience pride when they succeed in reaching work goals.[15] It is also in accordance with R. Sutton's and M. Chang's thoughts about appraisal determinants of teacher emotions and burnout, and with R. Pekrun's control-value theory of achievement emotions described in Chapter 3.[12,23]

There are four broad themes that guide teachers' formation of classroom goals and their perceptions of students' behavior: cognitive, motivational, social-emotional, and relational. The cognitive theme refers to students' acquisition of subject-specific competencies. The motivational theme pertains to students' motivational engagement in classroom activities and learning content. The social-emotional theme concerns students' development of competencies to respect themselves and others and to function within a social group. Finally, the relational theme pertains to the establishment of good relationships between the teacher and the students. For example, a teacher's goal might be that her students are able to correctly answer questions about a topic (subject-specific competence), show interest in the discussed topic and actively participate in class (motivational engagement), abide by the classroom rules (social-emotional behavior), or rely on her for answering questions and resolving problems (relationship with the teacher).

Five types of appraisals may be particularly important for teachers' emotions (see the middle, light grey section of Figure 4.1). A first and key appraisal pertains to whether or not teachers perceive their students' behaviors to match the teachers' goals or, in other words, if teachers feel they succeeded in meeting their goals (appraisals of goal congruency). The other appraisals include (2) appraisals of goal conduciveness, which examine whether student behavior is perceived as contributing to achieving a classroom goal (i.e., to approaching goal attainment even if not directly achieving it yet), (3) appraisals of coping potential, which evaluate whether teachers feel capable of attaining and optimizing their goals, (4) appraisals of responsibility, which correspond to the question of who is responsible if a goal is achieved or not, and (5) appraisals of goal importance, which examine how important it is for teachers to attain a particular goal or to avoid its non-attainment.

Teachers' emotional reactions are expected to depend on these appraisals. Generally, appraisals of goal congruency and goal conduciveness should determine the valence of the emotions experienced (positive vs. negative). Goal importance should determine the intensity of the emotional experience, with higher relevance typically leading to higher intensity for both positive and negative emotions (boredom is a notable exception, since boredom is assumed to increase as relevance decreases; see Chapter 3). Appraisals of coping potential and responsibility should determine both the valence and the intensity of the experienced emotion.

For an emotion to arise, not all of these appraisals need to be processed. Rather, there are characteristic appraisal patterns for different emotions. For example, anxiety should result from appraisals of low goal congruency or conduciveness, paired with low coping potential. More specifically, a teacher may react anxiously if he or she has the impression that many students misbehave in class (failure to attain the social-emotional goal that students should abide by classroom rules), and that this is due to his or her lack of classroom management skills (self-responsibility), while also not knowing how to establish better classroom management (low coping potential).

Empirical research confirms that personal doubts about their ability to provide effective instruction can be a cause for teachers' negative emotions. Lack of familiarity with one's subject has been reported to be a key source of shame for teachers.[27] Furthermore, teachers are often concerned about their ability to maintain discipline in the classroom and to use corrective measures to be taken in case of mistakes. These findings have more recently been confirmed by S. Intrator, who found that new teachers experience anxiety over lack of familiarity with the subject matter.[41] Conversely, teachers' judgments of their capabilities to produce desired educational outcomes in their students, referred to as teacher efficacy in the literature,[42] can be a source of positive emotions for teachers. For example, M. Kunter and colleagues reported a strong positive link between teaching self-efficacy and teaching enjoyment.[35] Similarly, in a diary study of math teachers' emotions, E. Becker et al. found that teachers' enjoyment of teaching related positively to their perceptions of efficacy and control ("In this lesson, I felt like I had everything under control").[43]

Students' Achievement Behavior

Research clearly indicates a link between students' achievement behavior and their teachers' emotions. Much of the available empirical data support the assumption that high achievement by students can serve as a source of positive experiences for teachers. In reviewing D. Lortie's work and reporting about teacher interviews on emotions, A. Hargreaves concluded that a key source of teachers' positive emotional experiences is student success.[44] For example, Hargreaves cites one teacher who said, "I feel very proud when they come back and say, 'We're doing very well. We've got good marks.'... So I feel very good about that" ([44] p. 843). Consistent with this, research has found positive relations between teacher-perceived student performance and teachers' enjoyment.[12] Conversely, a number of studies suggest that poor achievement by students can be a cause for negative emotions in teachers. Specifically, as noted earlier, anger is aroused if teachers perceive that their students' failure was caused by factors within the students' control, such as lack of effort.

Finally, apart from student achievement eliciting positive or negative emotions in teachers, teachers' emotions can also boost or impair student achievement. In other words, student achievement and teachers' emotions can reciprocally influence each other. Empirical evidence for the influence of teacher emotions on student achievement was provided in a study by S. Beilock and her colleagues.[25] The study showed that greater math-related anxiety experienced by elementary school teachers negatively influenced the math performance of girls (but not boys). Moreover, the girls in this study were more inclined to subscribe to the stereotypical belief that "boys are good at math, and girls are good at reading," even a year after having been taught by a math-anxious teacher.

Student Misbehavior

Student misbehavior and disruptions during class can be seen as one of the key factors arousing negative emotions among teachers, specifically anger and anxiety. Anger in particular is triggered when teachers perceive student misbehavior as an intentional action.[4,13] A. Hargreaves concluded from his interviews with teachers that anger was caused by students' nonconformance with classroom rules, whereas N. Hart found that teachers experienced anxiety as a result of student disruptions in class.[44,45] M. Chang and H. Davis studied teachers' self-reported emotional responses to disruptive classroom behavior and found that teachers' judgments regarding student behaviors influenced the unpleasant emotions they felt.[23] The emotional responses were particularly negative if the disruptions were perceived as impeding the teachers' classroom goals, or if teachers felt incompetent at stopping or curbing these disturbances. Studies by E. Becker, A. Frenzel, and colleagues also found substantial relations between teacher-perceived student discipline in the class and teachers' reports of teaching enjoyment (higher with perceived better discipline) as well as anxiety and anger (lower with perceived better discipline).[13,43]

Relationships With Students

Teacher emotions are inextricably linked to the relationships they form with their students. Teachers find the opportunity to be deeply and personally involved with students satisfying and beneficial. However, commitment and caring can also become a source of difficulty for teachers because of the inherently unequal nature of the teacher-student relationship. Extremely caring teachers may even feel guilty when they are unable to fulfill all the needs of their students. Failure to connect with students can also cause negative affect or pose a threat to teachers. As one teacher in L. Goldstein and V. Lake's study asserted, "I do not think I could deal with a classroom full of students who did not like me" ([46] p. 867). Beginning teachers, in particular, experience worries about whether their students like them.[20,41]

Adopting a quantitative approach, R. Klassen and colleagues studied the link between teacher-student relationships and teacher engagement as well as teaching emotions based on self-report data from over 600 in-service teachers.[47] They found that relationships with students are more relevant to teacher experiences than their relationships with colleagues. Teacher self-reported relatedness with their students was positively associated with their teaching enjoyment and negatively associated with their teaching anger and teaching anxiety. Similarly, in a study with Austrian secondary school teachers, it was found that the closeness teachers perceived in their relationship with students related positively to their enjoyment and negatively to their anger and anxiety.[48]

Effects of Teacher Emotions

Teachers' emotions influence their instructional behavior (lower, dark grey section of Figure 4.1). Once teachers begin to experience emotions, effects are bound to unfold regardless of how well they may later regulate these emotions. Specifically, teachers' emotions affect their behavior in terms of the cognitive and motivational stimulation, classroom management, and social support they provide.

A specific mechanism involved in eliciting effects of teacher emotions is the expressive component of the emotions. Emotions have a deep-rooted communicative function and, as such, are related to characteristic facial features and postures. Therefore, emotions experienced by teachers cannot go unnoticed by their students, except if their expression is fully suppressed.[11] As a consequence, the motivational stimulation a teacher provides (e.g., through displaying more or less enthusiasm) should depend on the teacher's emotional experiences during teaching. It is likely that emotional contagion, a term originally coined for dyads, plays a major role in this process, as outlined in Chapter 3.[49]

Other mechanisms through which teacher emotions are likely to be influential can be derived from experimental mood research. As explained in Chapter 2, positive and negative moods are associated with different cognitive processing styles. A negative mood is associated with convergent, analytical, and detail-oriented thinking. In contrast, a positive mood is associated with divergent, heuristic ways of thinking that enable more flexible and creative approaches. In the field of positive psychology, B. Fredrickson proposed that the experience of joy broadens one's action repertoire (**broaden-and-build theory** of positive emotions).[50] According to this theory, positive emotions not only indicate success but also produce or promote success by broadening thinking and facilitating the generation of ideas when faced with obstacles.

In Chapter 2, we described the relevance of these effects for students' learning. For teachers, this implies that teachers with positive emotional experiences may be able to effectively utilize a broad range of teaching strategies. These teachers are possibly more creative in class, more open to using "riskier" (e.g., less traditional) teaching strategies, and better able to flexibly deal with unexpected obstacles that crop up during class. As a result, they may provide better cognitive and motivational stimulation while teaching. In addition, they may also be more successful in building trustful relationships with their students. Conversely, teachers whose classroom experiences are dominated by negative emotions (such as anxiety and anger) may find it more difficult to deviate from the predetermined lesson plan and may use more rigid teaching strategies (such as rehearsal and repetitive exercise). A predominance of negative experiences during teaching can also be an obstacle to building good relationships with students.

Research findings confirm that teacher emotions are related to instructional effectiveness in terms of cognitive and motivational stimulation, classroom management, and social support. Teachers' enjoyment of teaching is positively linked to student ratings of monitoring, elaboration, comprehensibility, autonomy support, teacher enthusiasm, and teacher support for students. Conversely, negative relationships have been found between teachers' anger and anxiety and students' perceptions of teacher instructional behavior, including elaboration, comprehensibility, autonomy support, teacher enthusiasm, and support after failure.[8,13] Detrimental effects of teacher anxiety on teaching effectiveness as evaluated by supervisors and students have been reported by T. Coates and C. Thoresen.[20]

However, negative emotions can sometimes have beneficial effects (see the discussion of variable effects of negative student emotions on achievement in Chapter 2). For example, L. Stough and E. Emmer found that beginning teachers whose students showed hostile reactions to test feedback experienced negative emotions such as frustration and anger. As a result, some of them altered their classroom management strategies by structuring their feedback to better control student interactions.[51]

In summary, teachers' well-being, students' well-being, and the well-functioning of classrooms are related to teachers' emotions. Teachers' engagement in cognitive and motivational stimulation, classroom management, and social support, in turn, affects students' cognitive growth, motivation, social-emotional behavior in class, and relationships with the teacher—the "input variables" considered in A. Frenzel et al.'s model (Figure 4.1). As such, students' and teachers' behaviors in class can be viewed as both a cause and an effect of teachers' emotional experiences during teaching, as depicted in the reciprocal relations between these variables in A. Frenzel's model (see the reciprocal paths in Figure 4.1).

CONCLUSIONS

Teacher emotions are inextricably linked to classroom processes, including both student and teacher behaviors. As explained in this chapter, not only teachers' well-being but also students' well-being and the well-functioning of classrooms are related to teacher emotions. Typically, teachers' enjoyment of teaching relates positively to the quality of their teaching, whereas negative emotions can undermine the effectiveness of classroom instruction. However, little is known about how to support teachers in maintaining a positive emotional attitude toward their classes and teaching or how to break vicious circles in case negative emotions predominate the classroom atmosphere. Clearly, in future studies, researchers should make an effort to answer these questions.

Specifically, intervention studies are needed that show how to improve teachers' emotional experiences, not only for the sake of teachers' well-being and professional development, but also in the interest of emotionally healthy and well-functioning classrooms.

REFERENCES

1 Scott, C., & Sutton, R. E. (2009). Emotions and change during professional development for teachers. *Journal of Mixed Methods Research, 3*, 151–171.

2 Pekrun, R., & Linnenbrink-Garcia, E. (Eds.). (2014). *International handbook of emotions in education.* New York: Taylor & Francis.

3 Seidel, T., & Shavelson, R. J. (2007). Teaching effectiveness research in the past decade: The role of theory and research design in disentangling meta-analysis results. *Review of Educational Research, 77*, 454–499.

4 Frenzel, A. C. (2014). Teacher emotions. In R. Pekrun & L. Linnenbrink-Garcia (Eds.), *International handbook of emotions in education* (pp. 494–519). New York: Taylor & Francis.

5 Zembylas, M. (2003). Caring for teacher emotion: Reflections on teacher self-development. *Studies in Philosophy and Education, 22*, 103–125.

6 Hakanen, J. J., Bakker, A. B., & Schaufeli, W. B. (2006). Burnout and work engagement among teachers. *Journal of School Psychology, 43*, 495–513.

7 Maslach, C., Schaufeli, W. B., & Leiter, M. P. (2001). Job burnout. *Annual Review of Psychology, 52*, 397–422.

8 Frenzel, A. C., Pekrun, R., Goetz, T., Daniels, L. M., Durksen, T. L., Becker-Kurz, B., & Klassen, R. (2016). Measuring enjoyment, anger, and anxiety during teaching: The Teacher Emotions Scales (TES). *Contemporary Educational Psychology, 46*, 148–163.

9 Carson, R. L., Weiss, H. M., & Templin, T. J. (2010). Ecological momentary assessment: A research method for studying the daily lives of teachers. *International Journal of Research & Method in Education, 33*, 165–182.

10 Frenzel, A. C. (2016). *Emotions during teaching: Narratives collected from focus groups, diary studies, and interviews with teachers.* Unpublished manuscript. Department of Psychology, University of Munich, Munich, Germany.

11 Hargreaves, A. (2005). The emotions of teaching and educational change. In A. Hargreaves (Ed.), *Extending educational change* (pp. 278–295). New York: Springer.

12 Sutton, R. E., & Wheatley, K. F. (2003). Teachers' emotions and teaching: A review of the literature and directions for future research. *Educational Psychology Review*, 15, 327–358.

13 Frenzel, A. C., Goetz, T., Stephens, E. J., & Jacob, B. (2009). Antecedents and effects of teachers' emotional experiences: An integrated perspective and empirical test. In P. A. Schutz & M. Zembylas (Eds.), *Advances in teacher emotion research: The impact on teachers' lives* (pp. 129–152). New York: Springer.

14 Tong, E. M. W., Bishop, G. D., Enkelman, H. C., Why, Y. P., Diong, S. M., Khader, M., & Ang J. (2007). Emotion and appraisal: A study using ecological momentary assessment. *Cognition and Emotion*, 27, 1361–1381.

15 Lortie, D. C. (1975). *School teacher*. Chicago: University of Chicago Press.

16 Darby, A. (2008). Teachers' emotions in the reconstruction of professional self-understanding. *Teaching and Teacher Education*, 24, 1160–1172.

17 Keller, M. M., Frenzel, A. C., Goetz, T., Pekrun, R., & Hensley, L. (2014). Exploring teacher emotions: A literature review and an experience sampling study. In P. W. Richardson, S. Karabenick, & H. M. G. Watt (Eds.), *Teacher motivation: Theory and practice* (pp. 69–82). New York: Routledge.

18 Sutton, R. E. (2007). Teachers' anger, frustration, and self-regulation. In P. A. Schutz & R. Pekrun (Eds.), *Emotion in education* (pp. 251–266). San Diego, CA: Academic Press.

19 Liljestrom, A., Roulston, K., & deMarrais, K. (2007). "There is no place for feeling like this in the workplace:" Women teachers' anger in school settings. In P. A. Schutz & R. Pekrun (Eds.), *Emotion in education* (pp. 275–292). San Diego, CA: Academic Press.

20 Coates, T. J., & Thoresen, C. E. (1976). Teacher anxiety: A review with recommendations. *Review of Educational Research*, 46, 159–184.

21 Keavney, G., & Sinclair, K. E. (1978). Teacher concerns and teacher anxiety: A neglected topic of classroom research. *Review of Educational Research*, 48, 273–290.

22 Bullough, R. V., Jr., Bullough, D. A. M., & Mayes, P. B. (2006). Getting in touch: Dreaming, the emotions and the work of teaching. *Teachers and Teaching: Theory and Practice*, 12, 193–208.

23 Chang, M. L., & Davis, H. A. (2009). Understanding the role of teacher appraisals in shaping the dynamics of their relationships with students: Deconstructing teachers´ judgement of disruptive behavior/students. In P. A. Schutz & M. Zembylas (Eds.), *Advances in teacher emotion research: The impact on teachers' lives* (pp. 95–127). New York: Springer.

24 Adams, S., Heywood, J. S., & Rothstein, R. (Eds.). (2009). *Teachers, performance pay, and accountability: What education should learn from other sectors* (Vol. 1). Washington, DC: Economic Policy Institute.

25 Beilock, S. L., Gunderson, E. A., Ramirez, G., & Levine, S. L. (2010). Female teachers' math anxiety affects girls' math achievement. *Proceedings of the National Academy of Sciences*, 107, 1860–1863.

26 Hargeaves, A., & Tucker, E. (1991). Teaching and guilt: Exploring the feelings of teaching. *Teaching and Teacher Education*, 7, 491–505.

27 Bibby, T. (2002). Shame: An emotional response to doing mathematics as an adult and a teacher. *British Educational Research Journal*, 28, 705–721.

28 Goetz, T., Becker, E. S., Bieg, M., Keller, M. M., Frenzel, A. C., & Hall, N. C. (2015). The glass half empty: How emotional exhaustion affects the state-trait discrepancy in self-reports of teaching emotions. *PLoS ONE*, 10(9): e0137441.

29 Weiner, B. (2007). Examining emotional diversity in the classroom: An attribution theorist considers the moral emotions. In P. A. Schutz & R. Pekrun (Eds.), *Emotion in education* (pp. 75–88). San Diego, CA: Academic Press.

30 Morris, J. A., & Feldman, D. C. (1996). The dimensions, antecedents and consequences of emotional labor. *Academy of Management Review*, 21, 986–1010.

31 Schutz, P. A., Cross, D. I., Hong, J. Y., & Osbon, J. N. (2007). Teacher identities, beliefs, and goals related to emotions. In P. A. Schutz & R. Pekrun (Eds.), *Emotion in education* (pp. 223–241). London: Elsevier.

32 Sutton, R. E. (2004). Emotional regulation goals and strategies of teachers. *Social Psychology of Education*, 7, 379–398.

33 Philipp, A., & Schüpbach, H. (2010). Longitudinal effects of emotional labour on emotional exhaustion and dedication of teachers. *Journal of Occupational Health Psychology*, 15, 494–504.

34 Keller, M. M., Hoy, A. E., Goetz, T., & Frenzel, A. C. (2016). Teacher enthusiasm: Reviewing and redefining a complex construct. *Educational Psychology Review*, 27, 743–769.

35 Kunter, M., Frenzel, A. C., Nagy, G., Baumert, J., & Pekrun, R. (2011). Teacher enthusiasm: Dimensionality and context specificity. *Contemporary Educational Psychology*, 36, 289–301.

36 Frenzel, A. C., Goetz, T., Lüdtke, O., Pekrun, R., & Sutton, R. (2009). Emotional transmission in the classroom: Exploring the relationship between teacher and student enjoyment. *Journal of Educational Psychology*, 101, 705–716.

37 Wang, H., Hall, N. C., Goetz, T., & Frenzel, A. C. (2016). Teachers' goal orientations: Effects on classroom goal structures and emotions. *British Journal of Educational Psychology*, 87, 90–107.

38 Butler, R. (2007). Teachers' achievement goal orientations and associations with teachers' help seeking: Examination of a novel approach to teacher motivation. *Journal of Educational Psychology*, 99, 241–252.

39 Butler, R. (in press). Striving to connect: Extending an achievement goal approach to teacher motivation to include relational goals for teaching. *Journal of Educational Psychology*.

40 Jacob, B., Frenzel, A. C., & Stephens, E. J. (2017). Good teaching feels good—But what is "good teaching"? Exploring teachers' definitions of teaching success in mathematics. *ZDM Mathematics Education*, 49, 461–473.

41 Intrator, S. (2006). Beginning teachers and emotional drama in the classroom. *Journal of Teacher Education*, 57, 232–239.

42 Woolfolk Hoy, A. (2004). The educational psychology of teacher efficacy. *Educational Psychology Review*, 16, 153–176.

43 Becker, E. S., Keller, M. M., Goetz, T., Frenzel, A. C., & Taxer, J. L. (2015). Antecedents of teachers' emotions in the classroom: An intraindividual approach. *Frontiers in Psychology*, 6, 635.

44 Hargreaves, A. (2000). Mixed emotions: Teachers' perceptions of their interactions with students. *Teaching and Teacher Education*, 16, 811–826.

45 Hart, N. I. (1987). Student teachers' anxieties: Four measured factors and their relationships to pupil disruption in class. *Educational Research*, 29, 12–18.

46 Goldstein, L. S., & Lake, V. E. (2000). "Love, love, and more love for children": Exploring preservice teachers' understanding of caring. *Teaching and Teacher Education*, 16, 861–872.

47 Klassen, R. M., Perry, N. E., & Frenzel, A. C. (2012). Teachers' relatedness with students: An underemphasized component of teachers' basic psychological needs. *Journal of Educational Psychology, 104*, 150–165.

48 Hagenauer, G., Hascher, T., & Volet, S. E. (2015). Teacher emotions in the classroom: Associations with students' engagement, discipline in the classroom and the interpersonal teacher-student relationship. *European Journal of Psychology of Education, 30*, 385–403.

49 Hatfield, E., Cacioppo, J. T., & Rapson, R. L. (1994). *Emotional contagion*. Cambridge, UK: Cambridge University Press.

50 Fredrickson, B. L. (2001). The role of positive emotions in positive psychology: The broaden-and-build theory of positive emotions. *American Psychologist, 56*, 218–226.

51 Stough, L., & Emmer, E. T. (1998). Teacher emotions and test feedback. *International Journal of Qualitative Studies in Education, 11*, 341–362.

Five

Implications for Practice

As outlined in the first chapter, students experience many emotions during lessons, while studying, and when taking tests and examinations. These emotions can be positive (i.e., pleasant) or negative (unpleasant), and they can be intense and frequent. All of these emotions can have strong effects on students' learning and achievement. Emotions control students' attention, influence their motivation to learn, modify memory processes and the choice of learning strategies, and affect students' self-regulation of learning. Furthermore, emotions are part of students' identity, and they affect personality development, psychological health, and physical health. From a practical perspective, emotions are important because of their influence on learning and development, but students' emotional well-being should also be regarded as an educational goal that is important in itself.

Given the research evidence discussed in this volume, what are the implications for educational practice? In this chapter, we suggest guidelines about how teachers can understand students' emotions and what they can do to help students develop emotions that promote learning and development, and prevent emotions that are harmful. All of these guidelines are based on empirical evidence. However, the degree to which guidelines on student emotions follow from firm evidence differs depending on the emotion. As discussed earlier, much of the existing evidence relates to students' test anxiety.[1] For this emotion, it is possible to derive practical guidelines that are based on firm evidence derived from a large number of studies. For emotions other than anxiety, the number and scope of studies is sufficient to establish the guidelines discussed in this chapter, but these guidelines are based on a smaller number of studies, and some of them may need revision in the future.[2] We will present ten sets of guidelines that are organized around three major issues.

- Guidelines 1 and 2 address the nature and diversity of students' emotions ("Understanding Emotions"; "Individual and Cultural Differences").
- Guidelines 3 to 6 address functions, antecedents, and the regulation of emotions ("Positive Emotions and Learning"; "Negative Emotions and Learning"; "Self-Confidence, Task Values, and Emotions"; "Emotion Regulation").
- Guidelines 7 to 10 address the role of education in modifying emotions, including the influence of teachers, classrooms, schools, peers, and the family ("Classroom Instruction, Learning Environments, and Teacher Emotions"; "Goal Structures and Achievement Standards"; "Test-Taking and Feedback"; "Family, Peers, and School Reform").

1. UNDERSTANDING EMOTIONS

> Emotions profoundly influence learning and achievement. Therefore, pay attention to the emotions experienced by students.

The classroom is an emotional place, as outlined in Chapter 1. Students frequently experience emotions in classroom settings. For example, students can be excited during studying, hope for success, feel pride in their accomplishments, be surprised at discovering a new solution, experience anxiety about failing examinations, feel ashamed over poor grades, or be bored during lessons. In addition, social emotions play a role as well, like admiration, compassion, anger, social anxiety, contempt, or envy concerning peers and teachers. Many of these emotions originate within academic settings. However, some of these emotions are brought into the classroom from life outside the school. These emotions concern events outside the school, but they can nevertheless have a strong influence on students' learning, such as the emotional turmoil produced by stress within the family.

As discussed in Chapter 1, four groups of academic emotions are especially relevant for students' learning: *Achievement emotions* relate to achievement activities and to success and failure resulting from these activities, such as enjoyment or boredom during learning, hope and pride related to success, or fear and shame related to failure. These emotions are pervasive in academic settings, especially when the importance of success and failure is made clear to students. *Epistemic emotions* are emotions triggered by novel information and cognitive incongruity, such as surprise about a new task; curiosity, confusion, and frustration about obstacles; and delight when the problem is solved. Epistemic emotions are especially important in learning with new, non-routine tasks. *Topic emotions* pertain to the topics presented in lessons. Examples are empathy with the fate of one of the characters portrayed in a novel, anxiety and disgust when dealing with medical issues, or enjoyment of a painting discussed in an art course.

Both positive and negative topic emotions can trigger students' interest in learning material. Finally, *social emotions* relate to teachers and peers in the classroom. These emotions are especially important in teacher/student interactions and in group learning.

All of these emotions can have a strong influence on learning and achievement. Therefore, it is important for teachers to understand and to deal with the emotions experienced by students. You can use your own emotional experiences to understand what kinds of emotions your students may undergo—remember the memories of the emotions you experienced yourself as a student. Alternatively, you can try to talk to your students about the emotions they experience. For example, group discussion in the classroom can be used to share emotional experiences.

However, be aware that any assessment of student emotions by educators can involve a conflict between the need to know more about students' emotions and the right of students not to disclose their emotions. Students may regard their emotional experiences as a private affair that they do not want to share. Specifically, this may be true for emotions that are closely related to students' self-esteem, such as shame about failing an exam. Therefore, it may happen that you cannot easily assess your students' emotions. In fact, research has shown that teachers' judgments of students' emotions can be very different from students' self-view. By the middle of elementary school, students have learned how to control the expression of their emotions, including social rules about when to disclose or not to disclose emotions in the classroom.

To deal with this problem, build up a trusting relationship with your students to enable them to share their emotions. Also, you can use depersonalized self-reports in which students do not disclose their identity. For example, you can use anonymous self-report sheets to get feedback if your students are excited or bored by your lessons. Alternatively, you can ask for the judgment of others, such as the student's parents. For example, this may be needed if you suspect that a student is suffering from high anxiety about a test that he or she does not want to talk about. Furthermore, a more systematic assessment can be performed by professional experts, such as school psychologists, who are trained to perform high-quality assessment of emotions. Generally, when using one of these options, care should be taken to achieve a reasonable balance between the need to help your students and the students' right to keep emotions private.

2. INDIVIDUAL AND CULTURAL DIFFERENCES

> Consider the individual and cultural uniqueness of students' emotions.

Emotions involve subjective experiences that vary between individuals. As explained in Chapter 1, different students can experience different emotions, even in the same situation. For example, one student may enjoy classes in history, whereas another student feels bored. These individual differences can relate to culture, ethnicity, gender, school membership, and class membership. For example, as described in Chapter 1, average test anxiety is relatively high in students from some East Asian and Arab countries compared to students from Western countries. Moreover, anxiety is higher in female than in male students.

However, the differences in emotions experienced by different students within one culture are larger than the differences between cultures. Similarly, as discussed in Chapter 3, the differences among female students, and the differences among male students, are larger than the differences between the two genders. The same is true for ethnicity, school membership, and class membership. Most of the differences between students are due to the uniqueness of students' individual emotions and cannot be explained by group membership.

As outlined in Chapter 1, students can also differ in how they react emotionally to different school subjects. One student may be excited by studying a foreign language but be bored by mathematics, whereas another student may be the opposite—bored by languages but enjoys math. The emotions experienced in similar subjects (such as native and foreign language) are often similar, but the emotions experienced in dissimilar subjects (such as languages versus mathematics) can be quite different. The differences between emotions in different school subjects become larger as students progress in education, and they are most evident in high-school students. The reason for these differences is that students' self-confidence and interests often vary across different subjects. Therefore, emotions that are influenced by self-confidence and interest, such as enjoyment of learning or anxiety, can vary as well.

Finally, emotions can change over time. Emotional stability over time also differs between students. For example, some students tend to always enjoy math instruction, whereas others are more variable in their emotional reactions.

As such, to understand emotions, it is important to know that emotions have both universal features and individual uniqueness. For example, when students enjoy a lesson, this is a pleasant experience for students around the world. However, the contents, intensity, duration, and frequency of classroom enjoyment can differ between students and may even be unique to an individual student. You should be aware of the fact that only a minor part of these individual differences can be explained in terms of culture, ethnicity, gender, schools, or classrooms. Because emotional reactions can differ widely, even among students sharing gender and class membership, it is best to avoid stereotypical phrases that relate to group membership, such as "girls are afraid of math." It is more useful to pay attention to the uniqueness of each individual student's emotions.

Furthermore, to understand students' emotions, it is necessary to consider that emotions can vary across school subjects and time, even within each individual student. For example, it would be wrong to assume that students always experience similar levels of test anxiety across subjects. In fact, it is not possible to infer from a student's anxiety in mathematics that the student would also be nervous about languages, or vice versa. Because the amount of anxiety can substantially differ between school subjects, it would be misleading to think of students as either being generally test anxious or not test anxious.

For these reasons, teachers should avoid using the stereotype that an individual student always reacts with the same emotion across different subjects and academic situations. It can be quite misleading to label a student as "anxious," "bored," or "enthusiastic" based on his or her emotional reactions to one specific school subject. Instead, make use of students' varying emotional reactions by identifying the specific tasks and situations that result in them enjoying lessons, and help students to build their capacity for experiencing positive emotions by identifying their specific emotional strengths.

3. POSITIVE EMOTIONS AND LEARNING

Promote students' curiosity and enjoyment of learning.

Positive emotions are emotions that are experienced as pleasant. Positive emotions can vary in terms of the physiological and cognitive activation (or arousal) that is part of the emotion. As explained in Chapter 1, enjoyment, excitement, hope, and pride are activating positive emotions, whereas relief and relaxation are deactivating positive emotions. For example, excitement increases physiological parameters of arousal, such as heart rate, whereas relaxation decreases such parameters. Positive emotions influence learning by affecting students' attention, motivation, memory processes, use of learning strategies, and self-regulation of learning.

The research findings summarized in Chapter 2 imply that positive emotions can have profoundly positive effects on students' learning. However, this need not be true for all positive emotions. Specifically, positive task-related emotions, such as enjoyment of learning, focus students' attention on learning, promote their motivation to learn, and facilitate use of deep learning strategies and self-regulation of learning. Overall, you can expect these emotions to have positive effects on students' achievement. In contrast, positive emotions that do not relate to learning can draw attention away and lower performance, such as a student falling in love, which can lead to a reduction in his or her academic effort. Similarly, deactivating positive emotions, such as relief and relaxation, do not necessarily have positive effects.

Therefore, you can help students develop their motivation and acquire competencies by promoting their task-related positive emotions. Teachers should make an effort to promote students' enjoyment of learning, excitement about learning materials, and curiosity about new knowledge (see Guidelines 5 to 9), but they should not rely on triggering positive emotions that do not relate to learning. To facilitate learning, it may not be sufficient that students are just in a good mood; rather, positive emotional experience needs to be linked to the task of solving cognitive problems and studying learning materials.

4. NEGATIVE EMOTIONS AND LEARNING

Prevent excessive negative emotions, but also help students to use their negative emotions productively.

Negative emotions are emotions that are experienced as unpleasant. Similar to positive emotions, negative emotions can vary in terms of physiological and cognitive activation (or arousal). Anxiety, anger, and shame are activating negative emotions, whereas hopelessness and boredom are deactivating negative emotions (see Chapter 1). For example, anxiety makes your heart beat faster, whereas boredom reduces such signs of arousal. Negative emotions also influence learning by affecting students' attention, motivation, memory processes, use of learning strategies, and self-regulation of learning.

The research evidence discussed in Chapter 2 implies that negative emotions can strongly obstruct students' learning. Test anxiety, achievement-related hopelessness, or boredom during lessons can lead students to withdraw attention, avoid effort, procrastinate in doing assignments, fail exams, and drop out of school. Negative emotions are a major factor that explains why many students do not live up to their potential and fail to pursue the educational career that would correspond to their abilities and interests. Moreover, these emotions also jeopardize students' personality development and health, and contribute to the high numbers of suicide attempts among youth in many countries—both unsuccessful and successful.

Therefore, you should help students to prevent negative academic emotions, and to reduce these emotions if they occur, especially if these emotions occur with high intensity and frequency. However, you should also consider that negative emotions cannot always be avoided when learning and that they can be used productively if suitable precautions are taken. Less intense versions of anxiety, self-related anger, or shame can even promote learning if students are confident in their success, and some amount of confusion about cognitive problems can facilitate learning and the development of more advanced knowledge structures within students.

Try to reduce excessive negative emotions in your students, but also create a classroom culture that enables students to use the energy provided by unpleasant emotions to promote their learning. The key to creating such a culture is to raise students' confidence in their ability to solve problems, to focus their goals on mastering the learning material, and to regard students' errors as new opportunities to learn rather than personal failures (see Guidelines 5 to 9).

5. SELF-CONFIDENCE, TASK VALUES, AND EMOTIONS

> Promote students' self-confidence and interest in academic tasks.

Emotions are influenced by many individual factors, including genetic make-up, physiological processes, early learning experiences, personal values, and cognitive appraisals of one's ability. Among these factors, students' self-confidence and task values are of primary importance for their emotions, as outlined in Chapter 3. Self-confidence involves positive perceptions of one's competence and control over achievement. Self-confidence provides students with a sense of being able to learn and succeed but also with a sense of being responsible for failure. Regarding task values, interest-related values are based on students' interest in learning materials. These values are also called intrinsic task values. Attainment values pertain to the perceived importance of doing well, and utility values relate to the value of academic engagement for obtaining outcomes, such as praise by parents or a good job.

Self-confidence promotes students' enjoyment of learning, hope for success, and pride about accomplishments. By contrast, lack of self-confidence increases anxiety and hopelessness. As discussed in Chapter 3, boredom can be induced by high levels of self-confidence that are due to a combination of low task demands and high competencies, or by low levels of self-confidence resulting from a combination of high task demands and low competencies. For example, gifted students may experience boredom during lessons due to lack of challenge, whereas less able students may experience boredom because they consider tasks as too difficult.

Students' emotions also depend on their task values. Enjoyment of learning is experienced when the learning material is perceived as interesting and valuable. In contrast, boredom occurs when the material is uninteresting and has no personal value. The perceived importance of success contributes to success-related emotions, such as hope and pride, while the perceived importance of failure contributes to failure emotions, such as anxiety, hopelessness, and shame. For example, if a student perceives achievement in mathematics as most important, he or she will experience more pride about success, and more anxiety and shame related to failure in math than in subjectively less important domains.

As such, it is important to promote students' self-confidence so as to help them develop positive emotions, reduce negative emotions, and deal productively with negative emotions that cannot be avoided. Self-confidence can be increased by focusing students' attention on their strengths rather than their weaknesses. Failures can be regarded as opportunities to learn rather than indicators of inability. Students can be shown to attribute failures to lack of effort that is under their personal control, rather than to external factors or lack of ability. Other measures include providing high-quality instruction and mastery goal structures (see Guidelines 7 and 8) and avoiding high-stakes testing (see Guideline 9).

Helping students to value learning is important as well. Specifically, it is important to promote students' intrinsic task values based on interest. Two important ways to foster these values are using tasks that relate to students' everyday life (called authentic tasks by some authors), and making clear to students how tasks that may seem less relevant in the short term can nevertheless be important for their lives. You can emphasize the relevance of tasks by relating them to students' current lives or to their aspired future lives. Alternatively, you can let students learn for themselves how academic tasks relate to their lives—for example, by writing essays about the link between these tasks and their futures.[3]

In contrast, emphasizing attainment value can be a double-edged sword. Increasing the attainment value of academic achievement can facilitate positive emotions but can also increase negative achievement emotions, such as anxiety. The reason is that both success-related emotions and failure-related emotions are promoted if achievement is perceived as important. If a student perceives good grades as critically important, he or she may experience excitement and pride when succeeding, but may also experience strong fear of failure before exams, as well as hopelessness and shame if the examination is a failure. Therefore, it is better to help students develop interest-related task values.

6. EMOTION REGULATION

> Help students to regulate their emotions using competence development, situational change, and reappraisal.

Students can use various methods to promote their positive emotions and reduce negative emotions. Alternatively, for the regulation of negative emotions and stressful situations, the term "coping" is used. As discussed in Chapter 3, emotions can be regulated by directly changing their symptoms (emotion-oriented regulation) or by changing their antecedents (competence-, situation-, and appraisal-oriented regulation). Successful emotion regulation presupposes abilities to recognize one's emotions and to select appropriate ways of managing them. These abilities are part of emotional competencies, which consist of abilities to recognize, make use of, and regulate one's own emotions and the emotions of other persons.

There are several ways in which emotion regulation can be used to help students. First, you can design your lessons accordingly, as addressed in Guidelines 7 to 9. Second, you can help students by informing them about strategies to regulate emotions and by practicing emotional intelligence skills, such as abilities to recognize emotions. **Social-emotional learning (SEL) programs** can be used to practice these skills.[4] Third, methods to regulate emotions are used in the psychotherapy of emotions.

When teaching students about strategies to regulate emotions, you should know that all types of strategies described in Chapter 3 can be successful. However, competence development, situational change, and reappraisal are often the most efficient. These strategies can be used before the emotion occurs, thus preventing negative feelings from developing. In contrast, emotion-oriented strategies are used when negative feelings have already been aroused, implying that it may be too late to prevent negative consequences from happening. Moreover, emotion-oriented techniques can have unfortunate side effects. For example, regulation of anxiety by medical drugs can momentarily alleviate excessive anxiety but lead to the students becoming addicted to these drugs. When considering a specific strategy, always reflect upon the balance of benefits and disadvantages.

When a student suffers from excessive negative emotions, consulting a psychotherapist can help alleviate the problem. Specifically, psychotherapy for test anxiety is among the most successful therapies available today.[1] Variants of test anxiety therapy target the symptoms of anxiety (e.g., relaxation training), lack of self-confidence causing anxiety (e.g., cognitive therapy), or underlying competence deficits (behavioral skills training; e.g., training to improve learning strategies). Combinations of these various treatments have been shown to be most effective for many students.

7. CLASSROOM INSTRUCTION, LEARNING ENVIRONMENTS, AND TEACHER EMOTIONS

> Provide high-quality lessons and learning environments, and make use of the positive emotions you experience as a teacher.

The cognitive, motivational, and emotional quality of classroom instruction and learning environments is extremely important for students' emotions. As outlined in Chapter 3, cognitive quality is defined by structure, clarity, cognitive stimulation, task difficulty, and the match between task difficulty and students' competencies. Well-structured, clear instruction and use of moderately challenging tasks promote students' understanding. As a result, students experience an increase in self-confidence and enjoyment, and a reduction of boredom and anxiety. Moreover, moderately challenging cognitive problems can trigger cognitive conflict that facilitates surprise, curiosity, and productive confusion to promote learning.

The motivational and emotional quality of instruction and learning environments influences the perceived value of learning, thereby promoting enjoyment and reducing boredom. Motivational quality involves providing meaningful tasks that catch and hold students' interest (see Guideline 5), giving autonomy to students to self-regulate their learning, and introducing social structures of learning that satisfy needs for social relatedness. As discussed in Chapters 3 and 4, emotional quality includes enthusiasm displayed by teachers that demonstrates to students that academic engagement is enjoyable.

You can use several methods to improve the quality of your lessons. Importantly, the same methods can be used to improve the design of alternative types of learning environments, such as technology-based environments. As outlined in Chapter 3, it is not technology itself that makes a difference; rather, it is about the cognitive, motivational, and emotional quality of how the technology is used. Five important groups of strategies are the following.

Cognitive Quality

Provide instruction and tasks that have high cognitive quality. This helps students to understand the learning material, to build up competencies, and to develop the self-confidence needed to enjoy learning and reduce negative emotions. High cognitive quality can be obtained by ensuring that learning materials and explanations are well-structured, organized, and clear, and by providing an appropriate fit between task demands and students' current levels of competence. In addition, provide students with cognitive problems that involve a moderate amount of cognitive conflict likely to trigger surprise, curiosity, and productive confusion. However, make sure that confusion is resolved before students become frustrated, bored, or anxious when they are unable to solve the problem.

Task Contents

Use contents that are meaningful to students, which helps them to develop interest and intrinsic task values. You can make tasks more meaningful by providing contents that are related to students' current interests within and out of school, including their leisure-time activities, and by providing contents that are related to students' future personal and career goals. Alternatively, if the relationship between tasks and students' goals is not sufficiently clear from the contents, explain them to the students (see Guideline 5).

Autonomy for Self-Regulation

Provide students with the autonomy to self-regulate learning in order to increase their enjoyment. Autonomy can be given to individual students or to groups of students, and it can include motivating students to self-define their goals for learning, to select tasks and strategies used for learning, and to monitor and evaluate their progress. However, autonomy should be matched to students' competencies for self-regulation. If students are not able to select appropriate strategies, autonomy can induce anxiety or boredom rather than enjoyment.

Social Structures

Create social structures of learning that help students satisfy their needs for social interaction, which can promote their interest and the perceived value of learning. Examples are partner work and group work. If student groups lack the competence to organize their work effectively, you can assist them in developing these skills by scaffolding their learning.

Teacher Emotions

Emotions are contagious, and they can be passed on so that partners feel the same emotion, as discussed in Chapters 3 and 4. Therefore, the emotions that teachers experience and display in the classroom can have profound effects on the emotions experienced by students. This is true both for positive emotions (such as enjoyment, excitement, and pride during teaching) and for negative emotions (such as anger, anxiety, or frustration). Positive teacher emotions can promote students' enjoyment of learning within the classroom and can have long-lasting effects on the value of learning perceived by students. Therefore, teachers should take care to show the positive emotions they feel about teaching and the subject matter, and make sure that they share positive emotions and enthusiasm with their students.

8. GOAL STRUCTURES AND ACHIEVEMENT STANDARDS

> Use mastery goals and mastery standards for evaluating achievement.

As outlined in Chapter 3, different achievement goals contribute to students' emotions. *Mastery goals* relate to mastering the learning material and to improving one's competence. *Performance goals* relate to outperforming others or avoiding doing worse than others. *Cooperative goals* relate to group achievement based on cooperation between students. By focusing students' attention on the learning activity, mastery goals promote their enjoyment of learning and reduce boredom. In contrast, performance goals promote emotions related to success and failure, such as pride, anxiety, shame, and hopelessness. Cooperative goals are likely to facilitate social emotions, such as collective pride in the group's accomplishments, sympathy toward other students, or anger at students who fail to show commitment to the group.

Classroom goal structures involve the goals that are conveyed by teachers and can be shared by students. When these goals are adopted by students, they influence students' emotions, as discussed in Chapter 3. Due to their influence on emotions, these goal structures can have a strong impact on students' learning.

Similarly, the standards used to define achievement also influence students' emotions (see Chapter 3). *Mastery standards* imply measuring students' achievement in terms of the mastery of learning materials and improvement over time. More specifically, two types of mastery standards can be distinguished. *Absolute* (or *criterion-referenced*) standards measure achievement in terms of criteria of task mastery, whereas *individual standards* measure achievement in terms of the difference between present and past performance. *Normative standards* are similar to performance goals; they measure achievement in terms of an individual student's performance relative to other students' performances. *Group-based standards* measure the achievement of student groups.

Achievement goals and achievement standards convey expectations about the type of achievement expected from students. In addition, expectations from teachers and parents about the level of achievement students should attain have a strong impact on their emotions. Excessively high achievement expectations contribute to students' test anxiety.

To enable all students to experience success, it is advisable to prefer mastery goal structures and mastery standards over performance goal structures and normative standards. With mastery standards and sufficient preparation, it is generally possible for every student to attain success. Mastery standards imply that the achievement of an individual student is evaluated independently from the achievement of other students. Therefore, if every student attains mastery, you can inform all students that they have been successful. Use of mastery standards makes it possible for each student to be judged according to task mastery and improvement over time, which lays the foundations for developing self-confidence and positive emotions among the students.

In contrast, when using normative standards, teachers have to tell some students that they have failed due to performing worse than others, even if all students have actually shown mastery of the learning material. With normative grading, good grades for some students come at the cost of poor grades for other students. Therefore, performance goals and normative standards can induce a competitive climate in the classroom—with these standards students must compete for success, and some students will fail by definition of the standard. Competition implies that some students can experience positive emotions, such as pride of success, whereas others experience failure and reduced self-confidence leading to anxiety, shame, and hopelessness.

In many schools around the world, normative grading is expected from teachers. Even under such circumstances, however, it is possible to use mastery standards to provide added feedback on learning gains. Furthermore, group-based standards can be used to provide feedback on group work and individual students' contribution to group accomplishments.

Regarding the level of achievement teachers want students to attain, provide clear expectations that challenge students. Clarity and challenge can motivate students to invest effort. However, make sure that these expectations, even if challenging, are within students' reach and do not exceed their capabilities.

9. TEST-TAKING AND FEEDBACK

Use well-structured tests, provide informational feedback, and avoid high-stakes testing.

The organization of tests and assessments, the feedback provided after testing, and the consequences of individual achievement influence students' emotions, as discussed in Chapter 3. If the organization, demands, and consequences of assessments are not clear to students, test anxiety is increased due to uncertainty about the possibility of failure and its outcomes. In addition, tests that involve high demands on attention can impair performance in students who are anxious about tests, because part of their attention is already occupied with worrying about failure. Anxiety can be further increased during such tests. For example, this may be true when creative essay writing has to be carried out in a limited period of time.

Feedback about achievement on academic tests is one of the most powerful factors in the development of achievement emotions. Repeated feedback on success can strengthen students' self-confidence over time and increase their positive achievement emotions, such as hope for success and pride. In contrast, repeated feedback on failure undermines self-confidence and increases negative achievement emotions, such as anxiety of failure, shame, and hopelessness. This is especially true if feedback on failure is coupled with the message that failure is due to lack of ability.

The consequences of testing shape the value of achievement, thereby also influencing students' feelings about achievement. Whenever educational and occupational career opportunities are made dependent on individual achievement, the perceived importance of success and failure is increased. Combined with the likelihood of obtaining positive outcomes, increased importance can strengthen positive achievement emotions, such as hope for success. Combined with the prospect of failing to achieve one's educational potential or of becoming unemployed after graduating from school, students can experience increased anxiety and hopelessness.

To reduce uncertainty, teachers should provide clear information about the timing, demands, and consequences of testing. Do not use surprise tests that have not been announced to students, especially if this testing has important outcomes. To limit demands upon students' attention that put test-anxious students at a disadvantage, you can use formats that reduce load, such as multiple-choice items. However, using such formats may contradict the aims of assessment, making it necessary to find a balance between fair testing and the goal of assessing competencies that demand full attention. In addition, anxiety can be reduced, and confidence increased, by measures suited to increase students' expectations of success. Three examples are providing choice between test items, providing sample exams prior to the actual exam, and providing second chances, such as opportunities for repeating exams voluntarily.

Regarding feedback on achievement, you can strengthen students' self-confidence and positive emotions by using the following four principles.

(a) Use mastery standards and avoid normative standards for evaluating achievement whenever possible (see Guideline 8).
(b) Use repeated feedback on success rather than failure by emphasizing improvement of performance, even if improvement is small, which can generally be done when using mastery standards.
(c) There will be times when it cannot be avoided, or may even be necessary, that students have failed to learn some materials. In these cases, make it clear to students that errors

should be regarded not as information about lack of ability but as opportunities to learn.

(d) Beyond evaluative feedback about success and failure, provide informational feedback about how students can improve their competencies and attain mastery. Detailed informational feedback, coupled with positive expectancies that mastery is possible, will strengthen students' confidence in their abilities, as well as support all the positive affective outcomes resulting from such confidence.

Finally, consider the consequences of assessment. High-stakes testing is defined as testing that entails serious consequences, such as decisions about students' career opportunities. High-stakes testing can increase positive achievement emotions in successful students, but for students who fail, it increases frustration and shame about failure, as well as anxiety and hopelessness related to the future. Therefore, avoid high-stakes testing whenever possible. Rather, create a culture of using assessments to gain information about how to develop mastery.

10. FAMILY, PEERS, AND SCHOOL REFORM

> Involve parents, take care of the peer climate in the classroom, and contribute to school reform.

The classroom is not an isolated island. Students are influenced by their family, friends, and peers, and the classroom is influenced by school and university organization and the society at large. Therefore, factors from outside the classroom need to be considered to promote students' affective well-being.

Parents are the main contributors to students' development of emotions during the pre-school years and continue to be influential over the following school years. Pride of success and shame of failure are shaped in the family from an early age. Parents contribute to test anxiety when they hold excessively high achievement expectations that cannot be met by their child, and when they punish the child for failure. For most students, the parents are more important than teachers or peers for developing an identity in terms of individual core values, including the value of achievement.

Peers also influence students' emotions in the classroom. Competition between peers for positive achievement evaluations increases students' test anxiety. Peers also influence the social emotions experienced in the classroom. Friendship networks in the classroom help students to develop positive social emotions, whereas aggressive behavior, bullying, and victimization among students contribute to depression and social anxiety in the victims.

Finally, the organization of schools and universities provides the infrastructure and boundary conditions that facilitate or impede the implementation of emotionally sound educational practices in the classroom. For example, school systems in some countries include between-schools tracking that is based on student performance and assigns students to different tracks after elementary school. In such a system, it is necessary to use high-stakes testing at an early age in order to identify the performance information needed for decisions about assignments, which inevitably contributes to the early development of test anxiety.

PROFESSIONAL ACTION—BEYOND THE CLASSROOM

To understand students' emotions, it is helpful to acquire knowledge about their situation at home and in their peer group. Specifically, with K–12 students, any attempt to help students develop positive emotions and reduce negative emotions may be more successful when supported by parents but can fail when it meets with opposition from the family. Therefore, involving the parents may be most important to support K–12 students' positive affective development. Specifically, you can inform parents about their child's emotional situation at school, and you can provide parents with information about how they can support their child's emotional development. In cases of severe emotional problems that cannot be regulated within the classroom, it may be necessary to contact both the parents and an expert.

The peer climate in the classroom and at university also needs to be taken into account. You can influence peer interaction and students' social emotions by organizing learning in terms of collaborative student work. You can promote mastery-oriented and cooperative goal structures among students by defining achievement goals and providing feedback based on mastery and cooperative standards. Furthermore, you can also take action to reduce anti-social peer behavior. Specifically, research has shown that teachers need to intervene to reduce bullying and victimization in the classroom. Paradoxically, attempts to increase the social competencies of individual bullies and victims have proven to be insufficient and can even further aggravate the problem. In contrast, whole-school anti-bullying approaches in which teachers play an active role have proven successful.

Finally, being aware of the impact of school and university organization, school leadership, and the education system can help you to understand opportunities and limitations resulting in classroom practices that benefit students' learning and affective development. Furthermore, it should be noted that education systems around the world are undergoing rapid change today. Whatever your role in the school or university context, you can contribute to productive change by making your voice heard and helping to organize schools in emotionally sound ways.

REFERENCES

1   Zeidner, M. (1998). *Test anxiety: The state of the art*. New York: Plenum.

2   Pekrun, R., & Linnenbrink-Garcia, L. (2014). Conclusions and future directions. In R. Pekrun & L. Linnenbrink-Garcia (Eds.), *International handbook of emotions in education* (pp. 659–675). New York: Taylor & Francis.

3   Harackiewicz, J. M., Tibbetts, Y. Canning, E. A., & Hyde, J. S. (2014). Harnessing values to promote motivation in education. In S. Karabenick and T. Urden (Eds.), *Motivational interventions* (Advances in Motivation and Achievement, Vol. 18, pp. 71–105). Bingley, UK: Emerald Group Publishing.

4   Brackett, M. A., & Rivers, S. E. (2014). Transforming students' lives with social and emotional learning. In R. Pekrun & L. Linnenbrink-Garcia (Eds.), *International handbook of emotions in education* (pp. 368–388). New York: Taylor & Francis.

Absolute standards   Standards measuring achievement in terms of task mastery (same as criterion-referenced standards).

Academic emotions   Emotions occurring in academic settings, such as teachers' teaching emotions and students' achievement, epistemic, topic, and social emotions.

Achievement emotions   Emotions that relate to achievement activities and achievement outcomes. Examples are hope, pride, fear, shame, and hopelessness related to success and failure.

Achievement Emotions Questionnaire (AEQ)   Measure of various positive and negative achievement emotions developed by R. Pekrun, T. Goetz, A. Frenzel, and R. Perry (published 2011).

Achievement goal   Competence-relevant aim that an individual wants to attain.

Activation   Degree of physiological arousal, as indicated by symptoms such as increased heart rate, increased respiration rate, or sweating.

Activity emotions   Emotions related to academic activities, such as enjoyment or boredom during learning.

Affect
Term with multiple meanings. Specific meaning: emotions, moods, and feelings of activation versus deactivation (being awake vs. tired). Broad meaning: emotions, moods, feelings related to activation, and constructs related to motivation, such as self-concept and motivation to learn.

Anger
Emotion comprising hostile feelings; thoughts about persons and events that generated harm or obstacles; motivation to attack; physiological activation; and angry expression.

Anxiety
Emotion comprising uneasy, nervous feelings; worries about possible negative events and outcomes; motivation to avoid the situation; physiological activation; and anxious expression.

Appraisal
Cognitive judgment of attributes, causes, or outcomes of actions, events, or persons.

Attributional retraining
Treatment to change causal attributions, such as attributions of success and failure, to increase motivation, increase positive emotions, and reduce negative emotions.

Big-fish-little-pond effect
Negative effect of group-average achievement on individual self-concept, all other things being equal.

Boredom
Emotion comprising feelings of monotony; mind wandering and thoughts about lack of stimulation; motivation to escape from the situation; physiological deactivation; and bored expression.

Broaden-and-build theory
Theory of positive emotions by B. Fredrickson. It is assumed that positive emotions promote creative, exploratory

thinking and an enlargement of one's action repertoire.

Burnout Negative affective state including emotional exhaustion, feelings of lack of personal accomplishment, and feelings of distancing oneself from the situation (depersonalization).

Causal attribution Cognitive judgment that an event is due to specific causes; for example, judgment that success is caused by ability or effort.

Circumplex model Model of emotions and moods that arranges emotions in a circle along the two dimensions of valence (pleasant vs. unpleasant) and arousal (activating vs. deactivating).

Classroom goal structure Achievement goals transmitted by the teacher or shared by students in the classroom.

Cognitive incongruity Lack of consistency between different beliefs or pieces of information. Cognitive incongruity is thought to prompt epistemic emotions such as surprise, curiosity, and confusion.

Cognitive therapy of emotion Therapy of emotions through change of beliefs, values, and styles of thinking.

Competitive goal structures Goal structures referring to performance goals. Achievement is based on normative standards (i.e., relative to the achievement of others). Individual achievement is dependent on the achievement of others.

Confusion Emotion comprising perceptions of cognitive incongruity; physiological activation; and confused expression.

Control-value theory	Theory of achievement emotions proposed by R. Pekrun. It is assumed that perceived control over achievement activities and their outcomes, combined with the value of these activities and outcomes, generate related emotions.
Cooperative goal structures	Goal structures referring to cooperative goals. Achievement is based on group performance; individual achievement is a positive function of the achievement of others.
Cooperative goals	Goals to contribute to and raise a group's performance.
Coping	Strategies to manage stressful events and negative emotions.
Criterion-referenced standards	Standards measuring achievement in terms of task mastery (same as absolute standards).
Elaboration	Learning by connecting information to other materials, such as contents previously learned or information from other domains.
Emotion	System of interrelated psychological processes including emotion-specific feelings, cognitions, motivations, physiological processes, and expressive behaviors. For example, anxiety comprises nervous feelings, worries, avoidance motivation, physiological activation, and anxious facial expression.
Emotion-oriented therapy	Therapy of an emotion targeting the responses that are part of the emotion, such as reducing physiological activation through relaxation training.

Emotion regulation	Attempts to change emotions, such as increasing positive emotions and decreasing negative emotions.
Emotional competencies	Competencies to recognize, evaluate, increase or decrease, and make use of one's own and others' emotions.
Emotional contagion	Transmission of emotions among interaction partners due to mimicking emotional expression and thus adopting the emotional feelings displayed by the interacting partner.
Emotional intelligence	Term with multiple meanings. Specific meaning: cognitive abilities to understand and manage one's own and others' emotions. Broad meaning: emotional competencies more generally.
Emotional labor	Effortful generation of positive emotional expression or suppression of negative emotional expression; often due to display rules in a given context, such as teaching.
Emotionality	Summary term used to denote the affective and physiological components of test anxiety.
Enjoyment	Emotion comprising happy, joyful feelings; positive perceptions and thoughts; motivation to engage in the situation; physiological activation; and happy expression.
Epistemic beliefs	Beliefs in the nature of knowledge and knowing.
Epistemic Emotion Scales (EES)	Measure of seven epistemic emotions developed by R. Pekrun, E. Vogl, K. Muis, and G. Sinatra (published 2016).

Epistemic emotions
Emotions that relate to the knowledge-generating aspects of cognitive tasks and activities, such as surprise, curiosity, and confusion.

Explicit emotion regulation
Emotion regulation that is conscious, amenable to reflection, and intentionally initiated and monitored.

Extrinsic motivation
Motivation to perform an action because of its instrumental utility to attain outcomes.

Flow
State of fully focused concentration on an activity in which individuals forget about time and nothing else matters.

Group-based standards
Standards measuring achievement in terms of the performance of whole student groups.

Hope
Emotion comprising hopeful feelings, thoughts about a desired future outcome, motivation to attain the outcome, physiological activation, and hopeful expression.

Hopelessness
Emotion comprising sad and hopeless feelings; thoughts about the unattainability of an outcome; motivation to give up; and sad expression.

Implicit emotion regulation
Emotion regulation that is automatic and does not require conscious reflection and monitoring.

Individual standards
Standards measuring achievement in terms of the difference between present and past individual performance.

Individualistic goal structures
Goal structures referring to mastery goals. Achievement is based on absolute or individual standards. The achievement

	of an individual student is independent from the achievement of other students.
Intrinsic motivation	Motivation to perform an action for its own sake (e.g., because it is interesting and enjoyable).
Learning strategies	Cognitive, metacognitive, and behavioral strategies to learn materials. Examples are organization, elaboration, and rehearsal of materials (cognitive); monitoring of learning progress (metacognitive); and investment of effort (behavioral).
Mastery-approach goal	Goal to improve one's competence and attain mastery.
Mastery-avoidance goal	Goal to avoid losing competence and not attaining mastery.
Mastery standards	Standards measuring achievement in terms of mastery of learning materials and improvement over time.
Mood	Emotional feeling with low intensity, relatively long duration, and lack of a clear focus on a specific event.
Mood-as-information approach	Theory of mood effects. It is assumed that positive mood signals that all is well, thus making it possible to engage in exploration and creative thinking, and that negative mood signals that there is a problem, promoting cautious, detail-oriented, and analytical thinking.
Mood-congruent recall	Facilitation of retrieval of positive material by positive mood, and of negative material by negative mood.
Multimodal therapy	Therapy integrating different therapeutic approaches, such as emotion-oriented therapy, cognitive therapy, and skills training.

Negative activating emotions	Emotions that are unpleasant and physiologically activating, such as anger, anxiety, and shame.
Negative affect	Negative emotions and moods.
Negative deactivating emotions	Emotions that are unpleasant and physiologically deactivating, such as hopelessness and boredom.
Normative standards	Standards measuring achievement relative to other students' achievement.
Object focus	Focus of an emotion on a specific category of objects or events, such as success and failure in achievement emotions.
Organization	Learning by structuring learning materials, such as marking keywords or writing summaries.
Outcome emotions	Emotions related to the outcomes of academic activities, such as hope, pride, anxiety, and shame related to success and failure on exams.
Perceived competence	Beliefs about one's competencies that are stored in memory.
Perceived control	Cognitive judgment that oneself, another person, or situational factors are in control over one's actions and outcomes; for example, judgment that one's own efforts lead to success.
Perceived value	Perception of the importance of an action, event, or outcome.
Performance-approach goal	Goal to outperform others.
Performance-avoidance goal	Goal not to perform worse than others.
Positive activating emotions	Emotions that are pleasant and physiologically activating, such as enjoyment, excitement, hope, and pride.

Positive affect	Positive emotions and moods.
Positive deactivating emotions	Emotions that are pleasant and physiologically deactivating, such as relief, relaxation, and contentment.
Pride	Emotion comprising positive self-perceptions and attributions to one's own abilities and actions; motivation to engage in the situation; physiological activation; and proud expression.
Prospective outcome emotion	Emotion related to future success or failure, such as hope and anxiety, respectively.
Reactions to Tests Questionnaire (RTT)	Multidimensional test anxiety measure developed by I. Sarason (published 1984).
Reappraisal	Strategy to change an emotion by changing the emotion-inducing appraisals.
Rehearsal	Learning by repeating and memorizing learning materials.
Relief	Emotion related to reduction of tension and stress; comprises physiological deactivation and relieved expression.
Response modulation	Strategy to regulate an emotion by influencing the psychological, physiological, and behavioral responses that are part of the emotion, such as enhancing or suppressing the expression of emotion.
Retrieval-induced facilitation	Enhancement of memory by having retrieved and practiced related material.
Retrieval-induced forgetting	Impairment of memory by having retrieved and practiced related material.
Retrospective outcome emotion	Emotion related to past success or failure, such as pride and shame, respectively.
Self-regulated learning	Learning in which goal setting, planning, executing, monitoring, and evaluation of learning are self-directed by the learner.

Shame — Emotion comprising negative self-perceptions and attributions of negative events to lack of ability or inadequate action; motivation to hide or to change the situation; physiological activation; and ashamed expression.

Situation modification — Strategy to regulate emotions by modifying situations to support desired emotions and reduce undesired emotions.

Situation selection — Strategy to regulate emotions by selecting situations that support desired emotions and reduce undesired emotions

Social-emotional learning (SEL) programs — Programs to generally enhance children's and adolescents' emotional and social competencies.

Social emotions — Emotions related to other persons and the interaction among persons, such as admiration, compassion, envy, anger, and contempt.

State emotions — Emotions that occur in a given moment, such as joy upon receiving a good grade.

Study-skills training — Training of study-related skills, such as use of learning strategies, to influence students' emotions, such as their test anxiety.

Teacher Emotions Scales (TES) — Measure of teachers' enjoyment, anger, and anxiety developed by A. Frenzel and her colleagues (published 2016).

Teacher enthusiasm — Teachers' enjoyment and displays of excitement about the subject matter and teaching.

Test Anxiety Inventory (TAI) — Multidimensional test anxiety measure developed by C. Spielberger (published 1980).

Test Anxiety Questionnaire (TAQ)	Unidimensional test anxiety measure developed by G. Mandler and S. Sarason (published 1952).
Topic emotions	Emotions that relate to the topics of learning materials, such as empathy with a figure in a novel or anger about political events discussed in class.
Trait emotions	Individual dispositions to repeatedly experience a specific emotion, such as a student's tendency to often experience anxiety before exams.
Valence	Degree of pleasantness (positive valence) versus unpleasantness (negative valence).
Worry	Term used to denote the cognitive component of test anxiety (worries about lack of competence, possible failure, and negative consequences).

Index

Note: Italicized page numbers indicate a figure on the corresponding page.